# NELSON AND THE HAMILTONS
## ON TOUR

*Horatio Vice-Admiral Lord Nelson, Duke of Brontë, at the age of 43, painted by John Hoppner RA in 1801, the year before the tour. Courtesy: Nelson Museum, Monmouth.*

# NELSON AND THE HAMILTONS ON TOUR

## EDWARD GILL

*He's come, the British Hero see advance*
*His country's glory and the dread of France,*
*Each patriot's bosom glows with warm desire*
*To view the Hero they unknown admire*
*Each in idea would he a portrait frame*
*A portrait such as suits with Nelson's fame.*

ALAN SUTTON &
NELSON MUSEUM, MONMOUTH
1987

ALAN SUTTON PUBLISHING
BRUNSWICK ROAD · GLOUCESTER

Copyright © Edward Gill 1987

First published 1987

British Library Cataloguing in Publication Data

Gill, Edward
Nelson and the Hamiltons on tour.
1. Nelson, Horatio Nelson, *Viscount*
2. Great Britain, *Royal Navy*—Biography
3. Admirals—Great Britain—Biography
I. Title
395.3′31′0924     DA87.1.N4

ISBN 0-86299-382-2

Typesetting and origination by
Alan Sutton Publishing Limited.
Printed in Great Britain by
The Guernsey Press Company Limited
Guernsey, Channel Islands.

# Foreword

Many people still see Nelson as Robert Bridges did:

> He standeth in stone
> Aloft and alone
> Riding the sky
> With one arm and eye.

But Edward Gill, in describing the course of Nelson's journey to South Wales, a journey undertaken at a time when the great man was rarely out of pain, held no command, was parted from his wife, and shunned at Court, has revealed aspects of his character which the Trafalgar Square effigy does not. How well Macready records the contrasting behaviour of Nelson and Emma in the Birmingham theatre; how quickly Nelson comes alive when he recognises an old sailor amongst the welcoming crowds; and how rapidly he produces a report on the state of timber in the Forest of Dean – page after page of acid comment, with hardly a punctuation mark. Such examples vividly illustrate one of Nelson's most important gifts: his absolute command of time.

By using documents and local newspapers, Edward Gill has compiled an illuminating account of Nelson during the last years of his life, surrounded by flattery and adoring crowds, knowing that his talents were being wasted, and waiting impatiently for another chance of immortality. Lady Londonderry recognised this when she wrote, after Trafalgar: 'Had I been his wife or mother, I would rather have wept him dead, than seen him languishing on a less splendid day – in such a Death there is no sting, and in such a grave, everlasting Victory.'

Keith Kissack
*Former Curator Nelson Museum, Monmouth*

# Contents

*Acknowledgements and Preface*      ix

ONE:    Into the Arms of Fate      1

TWO:    Merton – Hounslow – Maidenhead – Henley      13
     – Benson – Oxford – Woodstock – Burford –
     Frogmill – Gloucester – Ross on Wye

THREE:    Monmouth – Abergavenny – Crickhowell –      23
     Brecon – Merthyr Tydfil – Llandovery –
     Carmarthen – St. Clears

FOUR:    Milford Haven – Picton Castle – Haverford-      33
     west – Ridgeway – Stackpole – Tenby
     – Swansea – Margam – Cardiff – Newport

FIVE:    Chepstow – Monmouth – Rudhall – Hereford      47
     – Leominster – Ludlow – Downton – Pencombe
     – Tenbury – Wells – Worcester

SIX:    Worcester – Droitwich – Bromsgrove –      72
     Birmingham – Warwick – Coventry – Althorp –
     Daventry – Towcester – Dunstable – St. Albans –
     Watford – Brentford – Merton Place

SEVEN:    The End of The 'Tria Juncta in Uno'      81

*Appendix A:*    *First draft of Nelson's report on the Forest of*
     *Dean*      86
*Appendix B:*    *The Hamilton and Nelson Papers – Morrison*
     *Collection*      91
*Bibliography*      97
*Notes and References*      100
*Index*      104

# Acknowledgements and Preface

It is now twenty five years since I united with Eric Freeman to produce *Nelson and The Hamiltons In Wales and Monmouthshire*. Over the intervening two and a half decades I have continued to research the subject, taking in the whole tour through England and Wales, and although there is still much more to be done, I feel this is perhaps an appropriate time to publish the story so far.

Throughout these years, Eric Freeman has been a constant source of information, encouragement and help in the preparation of this new publication. As a broadcaster and the author of several works on Pembrokeshire, he has been eminently qualified to advise on the tour through West Wales, and I am deeply indebted to him for his invaluable contribution.

In the course of my researches I have frequently enlisted the help of Monmouth's Nelson Museum, and its former Honorary Curator, Mr. Keith Kissack, and I would like to record my thanks to him. Latterly, Mr. Andrew Helme has been the Museum's Curator, and I am also indebted to him for his enthusiasm and assistance in the publication of this book. My thanks are also due to Malcolm Pritchard for reading the manuscript and to Carol Puddy for many hours of patiently typing and amending the innumerable drafts.

I particularly wish to acknowledge the help given to me by Mr. John Vivian Hughes and the staff of Swansea Reference Library, Mrs. Patricia Moore and Glamorgan Archive Service, Miss Anne Rainsbury of Chepstow Museum, Mrs. Joan Evans of Dyfed Cultural Services Department, Mr. Nick Mansfield, Curator of the Cyfartha Castle Museum, the Local Studies Department of Birmingham Reference

Library, Warwick County Library, Northampton County Library, the Scottish National Portrait Gallery, Hereford City Library and Hereford County Record Office. Also to Mr. Roland Williams for technical advice on the Welsh phrases, to Mr. David Lloyd of Ludlow, Mr. Peter Egan of Harrogate, Mr. H. E. Frost Curator of the Dyson Perrins Museum Trust and Worcester Porcelain Co. Ltd., and to The Duke of Hamilton, The Earl Cawdor and Sir John and Lady Harvey-Jones for their kind interest and assistance.

Finally, I wish to thank the Monmouth District Council for encouraging this publication with a generous grant towards its production cost.

As the reader will gather, much of the inspiration for my book has come from the Monmouth writer, Charles Heath, and it is to his memory and to his beloved Monmouth that I dedicate this work.

Edward Gill                                    Trafalgar Day, 1987

# ONE

# Into the Arms of Fate

Of all the names that have been engraved in the annals of Britain's history, there is perhaps none more illustrious and romantic than that of Horatio Nelson. But it would be difficult, if not impossible to write or even think of this great naval hero without linking his name with that of his beloved Emma, Lady Hamilton, who also carved for herself a niche in the nation's history beside that of her companion-in-arms.

As well as being Emma's lover, Lord Nelson enjoyed the devoted friendship of her brilliant husband, the antiquarian and diplomat, Sir William Hamilton. Their friendship began in 1793, when Sir William was Britain's Minister at the Court of the Kingdom of the Two Sicilies in Naples. In September of that year Captain Horatio Nelson, then aged thirty-five, and a rising star in His Majesty's Navy, sailed into the Bay of Naples and into the life of the envoy's young wife, Emma. Born Amy Lyon, the daughter of a blacksmith, at Neston in Cheshire in 1765, after a somewhat chequered career Emma had raised herself from the role of Sir William's mistress to become his wife.

The seasoned plenipotentiary was clearly impressed with the young sea captain from the start, for after their first meeting Sir William announced to his wife that he was about to introduce her to a little man who, though he could not boast of being handsome, would one day be the greatest man that England had ever produced, and would astonish the world. When she first met Nelson, the twenty-eight year old Emma was still young and very attractive. Her fine features, blue eyes and long auburn hair, so frequently portrayed by the artist Romney, gave her a classical appearance that men found irresistible, and Nelson was no exception. By contrast, Sir William was in his early sixties, and looking forward to spending some quiet years in retirement. Thus began a romantic association which would be talked about, written about and speculated upon for many generations to come.

But however fascinating the story might be, it is not the lives of the trio in Naples, or even Nelson's heroic life and death at sea with which we are concerned here, but with a few weeks in the summer of 1802, when they holidayed together on a carefree tour through Wales and the midland counties of England. It was a tour that turned into a triumphant progress, with Nelson fêted and acclaimed wherever he went. *The Times* newspaper afterwards observed: 'If on the one hand, the Country owes his lordship a large share of gratitude for the brilliant service he performed during the war, no man had it repaid in a more ample degree.' The outspoken Emma summed it up rather differently in a letter to Nelson's friend Alexander Davison, in which she took a characteristic swipe at the gossips: 'We have had a most charming tour – which will burst some of them!' To Nelson's sister, Kitty Matcham who, with her husband and son, accompanied the touring party from Oxford to Gloucester, she enthused: 'Oh how our hero has been received! I wish you could come to hear all our story – most interesting.'[1]

In 1801, the treaty of Amiens brought temporary peace to a war-wracked Europe. It was, in the king's words, an 'experimental peace' which, as it turned out, was to last less than fourteen months. France, master of Europe, and Britain, ruler of the seas, paused for breath before resuming the inevitable struggle.

Nelson, now confident in the growing strength of the navy, was unimpressed by Pitt's political rhetoric and his

*Lady Emma Hamilton as 'Nature' by George Romney. Courtesy:
Eric Freeman.*

*Merton Place – Nelson's Surrey home which he often referred to as 'The Farm'. It was acquired on his behalf by Emma Hamilton, complete with furniture for £9000. Courtesy: Nelson Museum, Monmouth.*

claim that 'We have kept our resources entire, our honour unimpaired, and our integrity inviolate.' Contrary to Pitt, he argued that the treaty gave more to England's enemies than was wise or reasonable. Nevertheless, the country's desire for peace was undoubtedly very strong, and the treaty provided a weary people with a welcome respite from war. Perhaps the Whig politician Sheridan summed it up most accurately when he said: 'This is a peace of which all men are glad, but of which no man can be proud.'

Whatever his view of national need or private duty, Nelson was himself badly in need of rest and recuperation after spending so many years of his life at sea. Following his defeat of the Danes at Copenhagen in 1801, he sought the Admiralty's permission to haul down his flag and come ashore. Earlier in the year he had made the final break with his wife, an event that coincided with the birth of a daughter, Horatia, to his beloved Emma. With a catalogue of victorious sea battles to his credit, and well-endowed with honours, he looked forward to some of the peaceful pleasures of English country life at Merton Place, the house he had recently acquired in a Surrey village close to Wimbledon. Lady Hamilton had undertaken the arduous task of house-hunting on his behalf, and had skilfully carried out all the negotiations to purchase the property for £9000 complete with all its furniture, the usual practice at a time when furniture was specifically designed and made for the house. A delighted Sir William wrote to congratulate his friend on what he considered to be a real bargain, and sent the master of Merton the first news from his new home:

We have now inhabited your lordship's premises some days, and I can now speak with some certainty. I have lived with our dear Emma several years. I know her merit, and have a great opinion of the head and heart that God Almighty has been pleased to give her; but a seaman alone could have given a fine woman full power to chuse and fit up a residence for him without seeing it for himself. You are in luck . . . The proximity to the capital and the perfect retirement of this place, are for

3

your lordship, two points beyond estimation; but the house is so comfortable, the furniture clean and good, and I never saw so many conveniences united in so small a compass. You have nothing but to come and enjoy immediately. You have a good mile of pleasant dry walk around your farm. It would make you laugh to see Emma and her mother fitting up pig sties and hen-coops, and already the canal is enlivened with ducks, and the cock is strutting with his hens about the walks. Your lordship's plan as to stocking the canal with fish is exactly mine.[2]

The canal mentioned by Sir William, which flowed through the grounds, was in fact a branch of the River Wandle which Emma renamed 'The Nile'. Here, at what Nelson often referred to as 'Paradise Merton', the three could live together as the 'Tria Juncta in Uno', (Three United in One), Emma's amusing reference to the motto of the Order of the Bath, worn by both male members of the trio.

After an exhausting overnight journey from the Kent coast, Nelson's first sight of his new home was on a dark autumn morning in October 1801, brightened by the glow of an excited Emma who had mustered all her household, including Sir William to greet him at the door.

He was now Viscount Nelson of the Nile, and the Neapolitan King Ferdinand had created him Duke of Bronte in grateful recognition of his service to Italy. Shunned for the most part by 'polite society' in England, he dreamed at one time of retiring to the isolated and obscure Commune of Bronte in Sicily to grow vines on the fertile slopes of the volcanic Mount Etna, but in the end he settled for his little farm in rural England. Life ashore left the recently ennobled peer free to take his seat in the House of Lords, and to enjoy the company of family and friends at home. For her part, Emma delighted in the domestic role of running the house, caring for the fowls and livestock, and playing hostess to an unending procession of house guests. One of these guests was Nelson's old friend Lord Minto who, in a revealing letter to his wife, told of his dismay and disgust with the Merton ménage:

*Sir William Hamilton by Grignon. In the Hamilton Collection at Lennoxlove; reproduced by kind permission of His Grace The Duke of Hamilton.*

*The Hon Charles Greville, Nephew of Sir William Hamilton; he was responsible for building the 'New Town' of Milford Haven. Reproduced by kind permission of The Earl of Cawdor.*

The whole establishment and way of life is such as to make me angry, as well as melancholy; but I cannot alter it and I do not think myself obliged or at liberty to quarrel with him for his weakness, though nothing shall ever induce me to give the smallest countenance to Lady Hamilton. She looks ultimately to the chance of marriage, as Sir William will not be long in her way, and she probably indulges a hope that she may survive Lady Nelson; in the meanwhile she and Sir William and the whole set of them are living with him at his expense. She is in high looks, but more immense than ever. She goes on cramming Nelson with trowelsful of flattery, which he goes on taking as quietly as a child does pap. The love she makes to him is not only ridiculous, but disgusting; not only the rooms, but the whole house, staircase and all are covered with nothing but pictures of her and him, of all sizes and sorts, and representations of his naval actions, coats of arms, pieces of plate in his honour, the flagstaff of *L'Orient*, etc – an excess of vanity which counteracts its own purpose.[3]

By the spring of 1802 poor old Sir William, now in his seventy-third year, was already beginning to tire of Merton's racy lifestyle, and he complained despairingly to his young wife of the interminable parties and constant stream of visitors – and of the expense:

I have passed the last forty years of my life in a hurry and bustle that must necessarily attend a public character. I am arrived at the age when some repose is really necessary, and
I promised myself a quiet home, and although I was sensible and said so when I married, that I should be superannuated when my wife would be in her full beauty and vigour of youth. That time is arrived and we must make the best of it for the comfort of both parties. Unfortunately our tastes as to the manner of living are very different. I by no means wish to live in solitary retreat, but to have seldom less than twelve or fourteen at table, and those varying continually, is coming back to what was so irksome to me in Italy during the latter years of my residence in that country. I have no connections out of my own family. I have no complaints to make, but feel that the whole attention of my

5

wife is given to Ld. N. and his interest at Merton. I well know the purity of Ld. N's friendship for Emma and me, and I know how very uncomfortable it would make his L'ship our best friend, if a separation shou'd take place, and am therefore determined to do all in my power to prevent such an extremity, which would be essentially detrimental to all parties, but wou'd be more sensibly felt by our dear friend than by us. Provided that our expenses in housekeeping do not encrease beyond measure (of which I must own I see some danger) I am willing to go on upon our present footing.[4]

Emma's domestic accounts confirm that her husband's concern about the escalating cost of housekeeping was not ill-founded. They also serve to correct Lord Minto's mistaken impression that Merton was being run at Nelson's expense, as an extract from the accounts shows.

Weekly Account of the Rt. Hon. Sir Wm. Hamilton and the Rt. Hon. Lord Viscount Nelson from 4th to 10th Oct 1802.

|  | £ | s | d |
|---|---|---|---|
| Mr. Haines, Poulterer | 7 | 9 | 6 |
| Mr. Stinton, Grocer | 4 | 19 | 8 |
| Mr. Coleman, Fishmonger | 4 | 0 | 8 |
| Mr. Wyld, Cheesemonger | 2 | 7 | 8½ |
| Mr. Scott, for Brown Stout | 2 | 5 | 0 |
| Coachman for Turnpikes & Expenses at different times from Merton to London etc | 0 | 15 | 7 |
| Mr. Gadd, Baker | 0 | 7 | 4 |
| Mrs. Cummings, for washing | 0 | 7 | 2 |
| Mr. White, for 4lbs coffee sent to Merton | 0 | 12 | 0 |
| To Richard for Turnpike at different times | 0 | 13 | 11 |
| Mr. Lucas, for Milk | 0 | 2 | 9½ |
| Mrs. Perry, Pastry Cook | 19 | 10 | 9 |
| Mr. Greenfield, Butcher at Merton | 8 | 12 | 10½ |
| Mr. Crib, for Vegetables at do. | 2 | 13 | 6 |
| Mr. Skelton, Baker at do. | 1 | 17 | 0 |
| Mr. Boyes, for Letters at do. | 0 | 16 | 4 |
| Mr. Woodman, Chandlers Shop at do. | 0 | 12 | 8½ |

| | | | |
|---|---:|---:|---:|
| Mr. Woodman, Publican for Charcoal etc. | 15 | 5 | 10 |
| Mr. Foottit, for Malt, Hops etc | 18 | 15 | 0 |
| Mr. Whitmore, for Poultry | 1 | 16 | 3 |
| Mr. Stone, Brandy Merchant | 13 | 1 | 0 |
| Mr. Bethese, for Fruit sent to Merton | 1 | 1 | 0 |
| Paid for Carriage & Porterage for 4 Hampers | 3 | 9 | 9 |
| | 111 | 13 | 4 |
| Expended at Merton by Mrs. Cadogan | 4 | 0 | 10 |
| do. in the town house from 4 to 11 Oct | 1 | 14 | 0½ |
| Total | 117 | 8 | 2½ |
| Last weeks accts brought over | 66 | 7 | 1½ |
| | | | |
| Total Expended from 27th Sept to 11 Oct | 183 | 15 | 4 |
| Paid Mr. White, Oct 19th 1802 N.&.B. | 91 | 17 | 5 |

Rec'd the 17 Oct 1802, of the Rt. Hon. Sir. Wm. Hamilton, the sum of ninety one pounds,seventeen shillings and eightpence.

Mercifully, the waters at Merton had been restocked with fish, and the ageing diplomat sought some solace in his favourite sport of angling – but he also had another absorbing interest. On the death of his first wife (the wealthy Pembrokeshire heiress Katherine Barlow of Colby, whom he had married in 1758) Sir William had inherited an extensive estate in West Wales, said to be worth more than £5000 a year. The property was managed for him by his nephew and Emma's former lover, the Hon Charles Greville, a younger son of the Earl of Warwick, who had some years earlier steered a Bill through Parliament to enable the development of Milford and its harbour. The ambitious Greville nurtured the hope that it would one day rank in importance with the great naval shipyards of Portsmouth and Plymouth, and in the person of Nelson he saw a powerful and influential voice to endorse the project and commend it to a Government with money to spend. If Sir William could get his friend to Milford, Greville would set the stage and provide the script.

Nelson is said to have had a particular dislike for Sir William's nephew, to whom he cuttingly referred as 'that other chap' who had used his lovely Emma 'ill enough'. When, at the age of seventeen, Emily Hart as she was then known, was thrown out of Sir Harry Featherstonhaugh's Uppark, Sussex home on account of her pregnancy, the opportunist Greville, then a handsome bachelor of thirty-three, took her in as his mistress, and her mother as housekeeper. Some years later both were to be disposed of to Sir William as part of a plot by Greville, to avoid being disinherited by his uncle's possible remarriage. Sir William, who had been a widower for some years, had a connoisseur's eye for a pretty face, and was indicating that he might now be glad of someone to relieve his loneliness. He had been paying some amorous attention to the eligible widow, Lady Clarges, whom he had first met in Turin, and then again in Rome where their friendship flourished. Anne, the talented sculptress daughter of Field Marshall Conway had also been the subject of his attentions. If he chose carefully, he might be fortunate enough to marry a wife who would bring with her a useful injection of capital to help finance some of the ambitious plans for Milford. But Greville saw Sir William's potential remarriage as a threat, for a young wife might produce a son and heir who would seriously threaten any inheritance destined to come his way. So the mercenary heir-apparent deliberately set out to divert his uncle into less perilous pursuits. When visiting his nephew at Paddington Sir William had frequently admired the girl he called the fair tea maker of Edgeware Row, and he was clearly warmly disposed towards her. It would doubtless be something of a sacrifice for Greville to part with his pretty young mistress, but it would be a small price to pay if it diverted his uncle from thoughts of marriage. In a long and persuasive correspondence lasting over a year, Greville set out to convince Sir William that he should take the lovely Emma as his mistress.

If you do chuse a wife, I wish the tea maker of Edgeware Row was yours. . . . At your age a clean and comfortable woman is not superfluous, but I should rather purchase it than acquire it, unless in every respect a proper party offered. . . . Your brother spoke openly to me, that he thought the wisest thing to do would be to buy love ready made, and that it was not from any interested wish, as he was perfectly well satisfied with the fortune he had, and that he should be very glad to hear you declare openly your successor, and particularly so if you named me.'[6]

Sir William's response to his presumptuous nephew was reassuring, yet cautious:

Was I to die this moment, my Will which I made in England with Hamilton of Lincoln's Inn and brought a copy here, would show that you are the person I esteem most – but I never meant to tell you so, as the changes in this life are so various that no one can answer for himself – for example, had I married Lady C., which might have happened, it must have been a cruel disappointment to you after having declared you my heir.

There was however, a hint of success for Greville in Sir William's reference to Emma:

. . . was I in England and you was to bring your present plan to bear, and she would consent to put herself under my protection, I would take her most readily, for I really love her. I think better of her than of anyone in her situation; but my dear Charles, there is a great difference between her being with you or me for she really loves you – when she would only esteem or suffer me.[7]

Sir William was still not totally convinced, and needed a little more reassurance, so Greville countered with yet another letter which seems finally to have met with the desired result:

She has a good constitution, yet is delicate, and I think her looks improved as well as her health. . . . I must add that she is

9

the only woman I ever slept with without having ever had any of my senses offended, and a cleaner sweeter bedfellow does not exist.'[8]

At length, Sir William was convinced by the prolonged barrage of persuasive letters, and he finally agreed with his nephew's plans for Emma to join him in Naples.

Having 'sold' his charge, the unscrupulous Greville's next task was to persuade the young Emma that a brief excursion to Naples would be beneficial to her. She could take her mother along for company, and in a few months, Greville would personally travel out to Naples to bring her home. It proved to be a hollow promise. Emma arrived with her mother at the Ambassador's Palazzo Sessa overlooking the enchanting Bay of Naples on 26 April 1786, the day on which she celebrated her twenty-first birthday, and within days was writing a tearful plea to her lover in far away England.

> I try to appear cheerful before Sir William as I could but am sure to cry the moment I think of you. For I feel more and more unhappy at being separated from you, and, if my fatal ruin depends on seeing you, I will and must at the end of summer. I respect Sir William, I have a great regard for him, as the uncle of you, and he loves me Greville. But he can never be anything nearer to me than your uncle and my sincere friend. He can never be my lover . . .[9]

In spite of Sir William's sincere efforts to make young Emma happy by providing her with all that she could possibly wish for materially, she continued to fret for her 'dear Greville'. Her new protector showered her with gifts and affection and she experienced the many pleasures and privileges of life at Court. She travelled, enjoyed the fashionable Italian practice of sea bathing, began learning to speak French and Italian, and even took music lessons from the finest tutors. Yet in spite of all this, she longed only to be reunited with Greville, and to this end continued to send him pleading letters:

I don't know what to do, I am now in a state, I am incapable of anything. . . . I am poor, helpless and forlorn, I have lived with you five years, and you have sent me to a strange place, and no one prospect but thinking you was coming to see me. Instead of which I was told I was to live you know how with Sir William.'[10]

Fourteen heart-rending letters were despatched before the heartless Greville broke his long silence. She received his first letter 1 August 1786 and, whatever it contained, it was not destined to bring happiness, hope or consolation to the unfortunate young exile who wrote back despairingly:

How, with cool indifference to advise me to go to bed with him. Sir William! Oh, that is worst of all! But I will not, no I will not rage. If I was with you I would murder you and murder myself both.

After begging Greville to write to her again, not as a friend but as a lover, she added a warning note that must have sent a chill through Greville's cold and calculating body, causing him to question his own judgement in sending the comely young maid to be his uncle's mistress.

It is not in your interest to disoblige me, for you don't know the power I have hear. Onely I will never be his mistress. If you affront me, I will make him marry me.[12]

In the course of time, she became resigned to her fate and perhaps decided that she would try to influence it rather than be its victim. She began to accept Sir William as something more than a friend, and there were signs of real affection in her letters to him:

I shall receive you with smiles and affection and good humer and think had I the offer of crowns, I would refuse them and except you . . . . Believe me I will never abuse your kindness

11

to me, and in a little time all faults will be corrected. I am a pretty whoman and one can't be everything at once.[13]

To Greville, she despatched an ominous note that could have given him little comfort.

I shall always esteem you for your relationship to Sir William, and having been the means of knowing him. I can never love any other person but him. This confession will please you I know.[14]

Her confession and what was to follow was hardly likely to please her former lover, for little more than five years after arriving in Naples, Emma returned to London with Sir William and on 6 September 1791 they were married at Marylebone Church. It was just two years before her first meeting with yet another man who was destined to change her life, and assure her of a unique place in history.

Emma had obviously acquainted Nelson with the unsavoury details of her unceremonious despatch to Naples, and neither she nor her new lover forgot or forgave Greville for his cruel deception. Not for Greville was Nelson prepared to make the long journey to Milford Haven, but for the sake of his good friend Sir William he agreed to fall in with the plan.

# TWO

## MERTON – HOUNSLOW – MAIDENHEAD – HENLEY – BENSON – OXFORD – WOODSTOCK – BURFORD – FROGMILL – GLOUCESTER – ROSS ON WYE

So it was, that in the summer of 1802, arrangements were put in hand for a large party consisting of Lord Nelson, Sir William and Lady Hamilton, and several of the Admiral's relatives to tour through the English Midlands and South Wales, aiming to arrive at Milford Haven in time to celebrate the fourth anniversary of Nelson's great victory at the Battle of the Nile on 1 August. It was agreed at the outset that Lord Nelson and Sir William would share the cost of the tour, and before setting out each contributed £100 to cover the day-to-day expenses. The total cost amounted to £481.3*s*.10*d*. and the detailed accounts written in Nelson's own hand are full of interest:

| | | |
|---|--:|--:|
| Horses from Hounslow to Maidenhead | 3 | 9*s*.4*d*. |
| Drivers turnpikes and gearing | 2 | 4*s*.0*d*. |
| Oyster Man | | 2*s*.6*d*. |
| Feed for horses and men at Pembroke | | 14*s*.0*d*. |
| Ringers at Narberth | 1 | 1*s*.0*d*. |
| Greasing the carriages | | 3*s*.0*d*. |

The tour has received no more than a passing mention in all the biographies of Nelson and the Hamiltons. Perhaps this is not surprising since neither Sir William nor Lord Nelson, who was accustomed to logging his daily activities at sea, kept any written record of the excursion, other than Nelson's own handwritten accounts of the cost along the way. But they were on holiday, so we are dependent on contemporary chroniclers, eye-witness accounts, newspaper reports and a few items of correspondence for our information.

On Wednesday, 21 July 1802, a happy and relaxed party set out in two heavily laden coaches bound for Oxford. The travellers consisted of Sir William and Lady Hamilton, Lord Nelson, and his brother the Rev. William Nelson with his wife and son, Horatio, who was on school holiday from Eton. Sir William was accompanied by his Neapolitan manservant Francatello, and Lord Nelson was attended by his valet, Gaetano Spedilo.

The first leg of the two hundred and fifty mile journey to Milford took them to bustling Hounslow, an important staging post for travellers to and from London. It rained incessantly as the carriages ploughed across lonely Hounslow Heath, where the sight of the gibbet acted as a chilling reminder that the Heath was a popular haunt of highwaymen. Continuing by way of prosperous Maidenhead and Henley, the carriages rattled over Magdalen Bridge in the late afternoon to make a triumphal entry into Oxford, through rain-drenched crowds straining to catch a glimpse of the national hero and the lady with whom his name was romantically linked. Bells pealed from every tower and steeple as the carriages came to rest outside the Star Inn, where they were met by Nelson's sister Kitty and her husband George Matcham, who had travelled with their son from Bath to join the party.[16] A few days earlier, the Admiral had despatched an urgent note to his brother-in-law telling him 'On Wednesday we fix to dine at Oxford. I wish you to fix the inn'. – This was quickly followed by a further note confirming the arrangements: – 'The Star Inn, Oxford, Wednesday 21st July. Dinner at 5 o'clock for eight – be so good as to order it, need not say for who.'[17]

It was still raining on the following day as Nelson, who loved to wear full ceremonial dress, walked splendidly attired and smothered with a glittering array of decorations

14

*'The Star Inn Oxford, Wednesday 21st July – dinner at 5 o'clock for eight, be so good as to order it – need not say for who!'*
*Courtesy: Oxford City Library.*

*Blenheim Palace, the magnificent home of the Dukes of Marlborough. Built by Vanbrugh, it was the present of a grateful sovereign to John, 1st Duke of Marlborough, victor of Blenheim. Courtesy: Oxford City Library.*

in a civic procession through milling throngs to the Town Hall, where he was presented with a gold box containing the City's Freedom.[18] Years later an old man by the name of Cox remembered how, as a young boy, he chased after Nelson through an admiring crowd, recalling: 'He was a little weather beaten man, but every inch a hero.'[19] On Friday, it was the turn of the University to bestow its honours in Wren's magnificent Sheldonian Theatre. The assembly of soberly dressed dignitaries contrasted sharply with the Admiral and Sir William, who were both decked out in brilliant and colourful attire, each wearing the red sash of the Order of the Bath for their installation as Doctors of Civil Law. Nelson's brother, the Rev. William, noted for being more temporal than spiritual, was made a Doctor of Divinity, which prompted the light hearted quip from the 'Morning Post' that with his knowledge of cannon law, it was perhaps Lord Nelson who should have been the Doctor of Divinity!

Since the death of Nelson's father in April the whole family had been in mourning, and the ladies were still wearing the customary black. The occasion seems to have prompted them to wear something brighter to match the gaiety of the tour and the colourful attire of the gentlemen, for prior to leaving Oxford they called on the local couturier, Dorton, in order to purchase some new dresses.

Well-satisfied with their reception at Oxford, they moved on to Woodstock and there spent the night quietly at a local hostelry. After breakfasting early on Saturday morning, the tourists went unheralded and uninvited to nearby Blenheim Palace with the intention of calling on the Duke of Marlborough. But there was to be no meeting between the Dukes of Bronte and Marlborough, for at Blenheim they were met by an embarrassing silence. For some reason, the Duke, who was known to be in residence, declined to receive the distinguished callers and instead sent a servant unceremoniously into the park with an offer of some cold refreshments, which were just as coldly refused by the visitors, who promptly took to their carriages and left.[20] It was said that Marlborough's apparent discourtesy was because he was a shy retiring man who disliked meeting people; but the real reason seems to have been the result of some recent gossip concerning the involvement of his son and heir with the wife of the member of parliament for Bridport. Like the Nelson–Hamilton association, it had been the subject of some sensational gossip in social circles, and he clearly considered one scandal at a time to be quite enough.

Sir William Hamilton observed indignantly that if the Great Marlborough could have risen from the tomb, he would have been eager to do the honours of his house to the Victor of Aboukir – a greater victor than himself! Lady Hamilton was outraged at what she regarded as an unwarranted affront to her hero, and consoled a humiliated Nelson with the assertion that the splendid reward of Blenheim Palace for Marlborough's services to the nation was solely the result of the fact that a woman occupied the throne at that time – and women had great souls. She went on to declare that had she been queen after the battle of Aboukir, she would have given her lord a principality to which Blenheim Park would have been but a kitchen garden. It was an emotional moment, and Nelson wiped away a tear as he took Emma by the hand, murmuring that he was content to have done his duty by his country and the people that he loved, and adding that he had not yet half done, for there were still two or three beds of laurels in the Mediterranean to be gathered.[21]

The gloom caused by the rebuff at Blenheim soon passed as they followed the gentle river Windrush through the blanket town of Witney to Burford, gateway to the Cotswolds, where the bells of the old parish church loudly proclaimed the hero's arrival. By 1802, Burford's wool trade was in decline, but being on the main route between London, Cheltenham and South Wales, it had assumed a new importance serving the busy coaching trade. For the local inhabitants, the highlights of each day were the comings and goings of the colourful stagecoaches bearing the legendary names of 'Magnet', 'Berkeley Hunt', 'Regulator', 'Paul Pry', 'Mazeppa' and of course the 'Gloucester Royal Mail'. That prolific writer on English rural life, William Cobbett, considered that after a fox hunt the finest sight in England was a stagecoach ready to start. But today, not even these colourful manifestations of old England could outshine the arrival in the town of the two coaches from Woodstock carrying Lord Nelson and his celebrated entourage. Amidst joyful shouts of acclamation from the villagers and townsfolk who pressed around the carriages in the steep High Street, they alighted at the Bull Inn, frequented in an earlier century by two other furtive lovers – King Charles and Nell Gwynne. The inn was well-known for its good food and warm hospitality, and its genial landlord, John Stevens, was eager to offer the travellers the sirloin and venison for which his house had become renowned.

After refreshing themselves, and with new horses on rein, the travellers continued over the Cotswold hills, past quaint old cottages sculptured from mellow local stone, and picturesque villages bearing such strangely evocative names as Lower Slaughter and Upper Swell. They crossed the Roman Fosse Way at Northleach, pausing briefly at the Frogmill Inn, then a lively coaching house on the peaceful banks of the river Coln at Shipton Sollers. Mentioned in Domesday Book, the Inn was once a mill that ground corn for the villagers, and brewed the ale for the 'communal feastings'. In these old coaching days when John Young was mine host, the 'Frogmill' is said to have been a very comfortable house, much frequented by dinner and pleasure parties, but revellers were reminded to obey the Rules of the House, prominently displayed on a notice board, the first three lines of which read:

> Fourpence a night for a bed,
> Sixpence including supper,
> No more than three to sleep in a bed![22]

The *ménage à trois* did not, however, stay overnight at the inn, and after changing horses embarked on the last strenuous pull to Gloucester.

The view from Crickley Hill looked down on the Gloucester plain, spread like a huge tapestry a thousand feet below, with the city dominated by its grey stone cathedral, rising like a sentinel in its midst. Beyond the silvery ribbon of the River Severn lay the Forest of Dean and the distant hills of Wales. The two-mile descent into the vale was a hazardous undertaking demanding considerable skill on the part of the coachmen, and for their own safety, usually requiring passengers to leave the coach and descend on foot. Having negotiated the perilous pitch, they approached the town the Romans called *Glevum* along the ancient Ermine Street, perhaps in a manner not unreminiscent of Ceasar's triumphal entry into the Eternal City. News of Nelson's impending arrival in Gloucester had already reached the city, so that by the time the carriages passed through the north gate, great crowds, feverish with anticipation, waited to escort them to the King's Head Inn on Westgate Street.

There was an air of carnival in the evening as Nelson and his friends walked through the city's narrow streets with the whole town in their wake to view the Cathedral, where a crashing peel of bells told of their presence. An eye-witness noted that Nelson appeared to be in good health, and clearly enjoyed the tumultuous reception.[23] So too did the entourage, but none more than the wordly Rev. William, who basked unashamedly in the warmth of his brother's popularity. Before returning to the inn, the visitors called at the new County Gaol where Nelson left a present of money for the inmates. It was a characteristic act of generosity by a naval officer, conscious that the rough and tough men who crewed his ships were often pressed from the imprisoned ranks of minor criminals. In this context, he perhaps recalled the words of Dr. Samuel Johnson:

18

*St Nicholas Church on Westgate Street, Gloucester. Nelson and his friends stayed at the King's Head Inn, on the extreme right of the picture. Courtesy: Gloucester City Library.*

*Gloucester Cathedral viewed from the west bank of the River Severn. Courtesy: Focol, Bath.*

No man will be a sailor who has contrivance enough to get himself into gaol; for being in a ship is being in a gaol, with the chance of being drowned. A man in a gaol has more room, better food and commonly better company.'

Having said goodbye to Kitty and George Matcham and their son, who were returning to Bath, the party left Gloucester before breakfast on the following day, destined for Ross on Wye. The road to Ross lay through pretty and undulating countryside of orchards and farmland, still cultivated with wooden ploughs drawn by oxen. It also skirted the Forest of Dean, in which the Admiral displayed a particular interest. He surveyed its trees with a mariner's eye, and like John Byng, who had passed that way some years earlier, he was appalled at the neglected state of the forest. In his *Torrington Diaries*, Byng had observed that: 'The woods are suffering and have suffered much lately from the axe, and can never recover owing to the flocks of sheep which prevent the growth of young timbers.'

By the time of Nelson's visit, cultivation had suffered even further, and such was his concern that, on returning to Merton, he submitted a report to the Admiralty on the state of the forest, in which he wrote: 'The Forest of Dean contains about 23,000 acres of the finest land in the Kingdom, which I am informed if in a high state of cultivation of oak would produce 9,200 loads of timber fit for ships of the line every year.' Like Byng, he complained of the deplorable state of the woodland and of the extensive damage done by deer, hogs and sheep. 'Vast droves of hogs are allowed to go into the woods in the autumn and if any fortunate acorn escapes their reach and takes root, the flocks of sheep are allowed to go into the forest and bite off the tender shoots.' Having identified the problem, he went on to suggest a solution. 'If the forest is to be preserved as a useful forest for the Country, strong measures must be pursued. First the guardian for the support of our navy must be an intelligent honest man who will give up his time to his employment, therefore he must live in the forest, have a house, a small farm and an adequate salary – the Guardian to have proper verderers under him who understand the planting, thinning and management of timber trees. Their places should be so comfortable that the fear of being turned out should be a great object of terror and of course an inducement for them to exert themselves in their different stations.'[24]

The report is a remarkable example of Nelson's acute powers of observation, analysis and concern for the defence of the realm, but it is unlikely that England, ever slow to prepare for her own defence, acted on his advice. Twenty years later the bucolic William Cobbett who passed this way on his *Rural Rides*, observed: 'Here is a domain of 30,000 of the finest timber land in the world, and with coal mines endless. Is this worth nothing? Cannot each acre yield ten trees a year? Are these trees not worth a pound apiece? And does it yield nothing to the public to whom it belongs.' Even the influential Samuel Pepys, who held high office in the Admiralty, had expressed dismay with the state of the forest following a visit in 1671. However, none of the visitors took into account the jealously guarded traditional rights of the fiercely independent Foresters – a vital, if somewhat retrogressive factor in the management of the Forest – when assessing the situation.

The unseasonal weather that had so far attended the travellers now gave way to more agreeable blue skies and warm sunshine as they neared the Herefordshire market town of Ross on Wye. Set quietly on the banks of the river from which it takes its name, it was described by Cobbett as 'an old fashioned town very beautifully situated – and if there is little finery in the appearance of its inhabitants, there is also little misery.' There was certainly little misery in the hearts of the inhabitants on that Sunday morning in July, when Nelson and his friends arrived at the Swan Inn.[25] As the visitors breakfasted, the ostlers were busily occupied in the stable yard, changing horses and preparing the

*An early nineteenth-century view of Ross on Wye from the river, showing passengers embarking on the pleasure boats used by Nelson and his party. Courtesy: Hereford City Archives.*

*Rooted in rock on the banks of the River Wye, Goodrich Castle is regarded as one of the finest of the border castles. Courtesy: Monmouth Museum.*

carriages to continue the journey to Monmouth. However, on learning that they could be conveyed by boat, all agreed that this would be the perfect way to enjoy the scenic beauty of the river Wye.

Perhaps it was 'Admiral' Evans, the self styled 'Commander of the Ross Navy', who persuaded the tourists to go by water, though one suspects that Admiral Nelson needed little persuading. The 'Commander' usually waited for customers at the inn with his boatmen, who carried the luggage and picnic baskets to the waiting boats. On that bright Sunday morning, a great concourse of townsfolk followed the visitors on the quarter-mile walk down Dock Street and through Mr. Walter Hill's garden to the river where a pleasure boat, garlanded with laurel leaves, waited to take its important passengers downstream to Monmouth. Charles Heath, who chronicled local happenings throughout the lower Wye Valley for over forty years, records that it was usual for the owner of the vessel to accompany passengers to the point of embarkation, '. . . so that the ear is not pained with the coarseness of language frequently heard from the navigators of public river!'

The colourful little pleasure craft were comfortably fitted out to accommodate up to fourteen people, on padded seating beneath which were lockers where provisions for a picnic could be safely stored. A gaily decorated awning protected passengers from the heat of the sun or inclement weather, but it is likely that on this occasion the awning was lowered to give everyone a better opportunity to see the great Lord Nelson. With its voyagers safely aboard, the little vessel drifted lazily downstream, beneath the ivy clad walls of Goodrich Castle, which looked for all the world as though it had grown out of the rock in which it is rooted.

They could leave the boat at Coldwell and, like most Wye sightseers, tackle the energetic climb to Symonds Yat Rock high above the river. Had they done so, their exertions would have been well-rewarded with the magnificent spectacle of the surrounding countryside, and an interesting view of the bold, sweeping course of the river below. On returning to the lower ground, it was usual in the summer months for tourists to spread a cloth and enjoy a leisurely picnic on that part of the river bank generally considered to be the most picturesque part of the valley. It was a stretch of water much favoured by coracle fishermen, who may well have joined the Admiral through the gorge of the Seven Sisters rocks on the final part of his river excursion. The winding course of the river from Ross to Monmouth covers some twenty miles, just twice the distance by road, but infinitely more comfortable and relaxing.

At four o'clock in the afternoon, the boat bearing its illustrious passenger came within sight of Monmouth at Hadnock Reach, where an armada of small craft of every description was waiting to escort it to the town quay. Nelson got up from his seat and made his way to the bow of the boat, where he stood bareheaded as it sailed between riverbanks overflowing with wildly excited men, women and children, all cheering their hearts out at the sight of their hero. The blast of cannon fired from the nearby Kymin Hill echoed through the valley, signalling the arrival of the victor of the Nile at the birthplace of Henry V, victor of Agincourt.[26]

*The small craft carrying Nelson sailed beneath the Seven Sisters Rocks providing a dramatic backdrop for this peaceful scene on the River Wye. An original oil painting by Willis Price in the possession of the author.*

*Wye Bridge at Monmouth where Nelson was received by the Mayor & Corporation as the band played 'See the Conquering Hero Comes'. From an original watercolour by Mary Bagnall-Oakley. Courtesy: Monmouth Museum.*

# THREE

MONMOUTH – ABERGAVENNY – CRICKHOWELL –
BRECON – MERTHYR TYDFIL – LLANDOVERY –
CARMARTHEN – ST. CLEARS

Nelson and his friends disembarked and were greeted by the Mayor and Corporation, with the band of the Monmouth and Brecon Militia playing *See the Conquering Hero Comes*. After a short speech of welcome by the Mayor, the party moved in procession behind the band, now playing *Rule Britannia*, through the town's narrow streets crammed with excited people. At the Beaufort Arms Inn, the Admiral spoke to the large, vociferous gathering that had packed into Agincourt Square. 'Had I arrived at any of the great sea port towns in the kingdom, I should not have been much surprised at this token of attachment from my Jolly Jack Tars, but to be known at such a little gut of a river as the Wye, fills me with astonishment.' At this his audience erupted with an even greater demonstration of patriotism as they spontaneously broke into a chorus of *God Save the King*.

With the noise of the crowds still ringing in their ears, the visitors withdrew to the 'Beaufort', and there dined quietly together. When dinner was over, Mr. Watkins the landlord invited his celebrated guests to accept some bottles of claret that had lain in the cellar for a number of years. The generous offer was cheerfully accepted and the claret poured by a proud landlord, who told Nelson: – 'I have filled many a glass to your Lordship's health, but never did I expect the pleasure of doing so in this present situation.' 'Where was I when you drank my health?' asked the Admiral.

23

'After the Battle of the Nile my lord', answered Watkins. 'Poh, that was nothing', replied the victor, 'I always did beat the French, and I always will, Watkins, whenever they give me the opportunity of meeting them; but I have had a harder day since.' This intriguing remark tempted the landlord to enquire: 'In what action my lord?' 'At Copenhagen' was the reply, 'that was a terrible day indeed.'[27] It was perhaps characteristic of the man, that this peer of the realm and hero of the age could, without the slightest inhibition, sit at table and talk to a simple country inn keeper. One wonders if it was this apparent ease of communication with ordinary people that contributed to the remarkable powers of leadership that earned him respect from the highest statesman to the lowliest seaman.

The little market town of Monmouth was not unknown to Nelson who, in his absence, had been admitted as a freeman of the Borough in the previous year. So in the evening, he took the opportunity to call on the mayor and thank him personally for this deeply-appreciated mark of respect. Mayor Hollings responded by inviting the visitors to stay on in the town and be the Corporation's guests at a civic luncheon on the following day, but as time would not permit, they agreed to stay longer on their return journey, promising to give the mayor three clear days notice of their intended arrival.

From here they resumed the journey westward, stopping only to change horses at Abergavenny, before following the Usk valley between the Sugar Loaf and Blorenge mountains to Crickhowell, and the home of Nelson's long-time friend, Admiral John Gell. Described by a contemporary as a 'rough swearing tar with a good heart', he lived in Llanwysg, an elegantly eccentric Italianate house on the banks of the river Usk, said to have been designed by Nash. Gell's principal claim to fame was the capture in 1793, of the Spanish treasure ship *Santiago*, reckoned to be worth over a million pounds.[28] It was an aggressive act that enraged the Spaniards, who promptly ceased hostilities against France

*Admiral John Gell of Crickhowell. Described by the historian Richard Fenton as '. . . a rough swearing tar with a good heart who could provide a good dinner and excellent Madeira.' By Permission: Trustees, The National Maritime Museum.*

*Llanwysg, Admiral Gell's Italianate house on the banks of the River Usk at Crickhowell. Courtesy: Mr. H. Bryan.*

and declared war on England. The two old salts had served together at the occupation of Toulon, and doubtless enjoyed recalling their Mediterranean adventures over a glass of Gell's excellent Madeira.

The road from Crickhowell to Brecon was winding and difficult but outstandingly beautiful, with breathtaking views of the Brecon Beacons. In the fine weather of high summer Nelson was now very relaxed, feeling the benefits of a much-needed rest. As the friends tripped through the Principality, news of their progress began to filter back to London, and brief reports appeared in various newspapers. The popular *Morning Post*, noted for its 'fashionable intelligence' quipped, 'Sir William's party are quite in love with each other in the Welsh mountains. They drink nothing but goats milk.'

At length, they arrived in Brecon, to be met by a deputation of local farmers. The sight of the battered warrior surprised these tough Welsh men of the soil as he stood before them. One-eyed and one-armed, with a disfiguring scar on his forehead, and little more than five feet two inches in height, his must have seemed an unlikely frame in which to deposit the heart of a lion! It was too much for some of them, who were so overcome that they broke down and wept like children as a spokesman stepped forward to address their hero. 'My lord, you have saved us. While you were losing your limbs and shedding your blood for us we slept soundly with our wives, and our land and children were protected by your vigilance. Accept our thanks; these tears will tell you how we feel.'[29] The local bard Walter Churchey, a friend of Nelson's biographer Southey, was himself moved to pen some commemorative lines in celebration of the occasion.

Hail Warrior! wounded in thy country's cause
I sing while sorrow tempers my applause!
While with kindling crowd my hat I wave,
With cordial zeal to celebrate the brave!

To greet the far famed Hero of the Nile!
Who scourged Usurpers for perfidious Guile,
Who linked with Sidney on the Egyptian shore,
Touched great Achilles' Heel – untouched before!
Who broke the massy Boom – the magic Chain,
Of Northern Powers – by thund'ring on the Dane.
Thus to retaliate – after many an age,
The wrongs Britannia felt from Danish Rage!
When England's Alfred – Friend of God and Man,
Our sacred Rights and naval Pow'r began!
While thus thy Martial Deeds and dauntless Soul,
In lines of Brass, to future Times shall roll,
Permit a peaceful Muse, for Wars unmeet!
For once to lay this Tribute at thy Feet!
While with a melting Sense, and cordial sigh.
On Nelson's wounds she turns a moistened Eye.
Forc'd from the chequer'd Scene thy Words to sing,[30]

Some days later, the poet was the proud recipient of a letter from his hero:

Milford                                              August 3rd 1802

Sir, I feel much flattered by your kindness and I may say with truth that my obligation extends to the whole town of Brecon for their flattering reception of me.

Should our party return through Brecon, I shall have much pleasure in thanking you in person and assuring you that I feel myself your much obliged servant.

Nelson & Bronte[31]

Following the rather touching reception at Brecon, they once again took to the road, but soon diverted from the route normally taken by travellers journeying west to make a visit to that cradle of the industrial revolution, Merthyr Tydfil, which Nelson refers to in his accounts as

*Crawshay's Cyfartha Ironworks, a cradle of the industrial revolution. Courtesy: Cyfartha Castle Museum, Merthyr Tydfil.*

*Richard Crawshay, the tough ironmaster who was moved to tears at the sight of Nelson. Courtesy: Cyfartha Castle Museum, Merthyr Tydfil.*

'Myrter Tidder'. Here, they were to call on the legendary ironmaster, Richard Crawshay, a hard-headed Yorkshireman who had amused and impressed Sir William when visiting the town in the previous year. In a letter to Emma, he had told her the story of Crawshay's rise from shepherd boy to industrial giant.

> Mr. Morris told me last night the history of Mr. Crawshay, who so hospitably received and entertained us at his house for two days and nights and shewe'd us all his mines and works – it is almost a romance. He was a shepherd boy, and guarding the sheep on a cold day in the mountains he thought he cou'd do something better – ran away to London and was porter to an iron-monger in the City. By his industry he became to have a small share with his Master, who having concerns in the iron works at Marty Tidwell used to send him there to inspect the works. He thought they did not carry them on properly, but as his master wou'd not alter his plan he broke (failed) and Crawshay was bold enough to undertake with his little stock to carry on the business and clears annual at least £30,000.[32]

Now he wanted Emma and Nelson to meet Crawshay and see the notorious Cyfartha foundry for themselves.

Merthyr was at that time the largest town in Wales, with a population well in excess of ten thousand, largely dependent on the iron works which employed fifteen hundred men. The arrival of Nelson and his party was quite unexpected and took everyone by surprise, including Miss Jenkins, the landlady of the Star Inn where they stayed. News of their presence quickly spread as men, women and children poured into the streets, all hastening in the direction of the 'Star', with the town taking on a festive air as shops were closed and a public holiday proclaimed. A number of young men formed themselves into a makeshift band and, playing *Rule Britannia*, marched to the inn where a large crowd had gathered, chanting for Nelson to make an appearance. When he

27

eventually came to an upstairs window, he was greeted by three rousing cheers and several volleys of musket fire. Each time they cheered, he bowed in acknowledgement and as he did so the noise grew louder and louder.[33]

Life in Merthyr was grim in those early days of the industrial revolution, with little to relieve the toil and drudgery associated with the fast-growing industries that were scarring the natural landscape of the lovely Welsh valleys. Here, they had produced guns for the navy's men o' war and Nelson was not slow to demonstrate his recognition and appreciation of their vital contribution to his great victories. His visit was like a breath of fresh air, bringing to the lives of these ordinary working folk a new sense of purpose.

In the evening there was plenty of laughter and conversation during dinner, with people peering through the windows to see the admiral at table. He had a remarkably good memory for faces, and one face he recognised in the crowds was that of Will Ellis, a local man who had served on one of his ships. He was delighted to see the old sailor and gave him a guinea to 'splice the mainbrace'.[34] He also offered a guinea to anyone who would drink his health in Welsh, whereupon Mr. Rowlands, the Parish Clerk, raised his glass to propose a toast in the mother tongue, 'Yfwn i arwr y Neil! Croeso i Cymru!' 'Let's drink to the Hero of the Nile! Welcome to Wales!' At this, Miss Jenkins produced a large mug which she filled with wine to be passed around the table so that everyone might drink the Admiral's health. The mug was finally passed to Nelson himself, who raised it up to drink a toast – and from that moment the modest vessel became the landlady's most treasured possession,[35] and it survives to this day in the town's museum. Celebrations continued well into the night, but were sadly marred by an unfortunate incident when a gun discharged accidentally, injuring three people and killing a young boy. Lady Hamilton was deeply distressed and insisted on seeing the child's parents, to whom she gave some money for a decent funeral.

*At night the fires from Merthyr's ironworks lit up the sky and could be seen for miles. From a watercolour by Thomas Horner. Courtesy: Swansea City Library.*

*Crawshay proudly conducted his visitors round his Cyfartha Works through fire, flame, smoke and ashes to the accompaniment of the deafening noise of powerful hammers. Courtesy: Cyfartha Castle Museum, Merthyr Tydfil.*

The tour was already proving to be one of sharp contrasts. Merthyr's flaming furnaces beneath their ugly smoke-belching chimneys, were a world away from Oxford's learned spires. But if the furnaces were warm, so too were the hearts of the people whose welcome would be remembered long after Marlborough's cold rebuff had been forgotten. Nelson was well pleased with his reception at Merthyr, but he had not come here just to be fêted; this was where the guns for the navy were forged, and he was eager to see it all for himself.

When the party arrived at Cyfartha on the following day, huge crowds surrounded the works. There to greet them was the great ironmaster Richard Crawshay himself, all dressed up in his best three-quarter length coat and knee breeches, with a spotless white cravat at his neck, and wearing a freshly powdered wig. He proudly conducted the celebrated visitors round the works through fire, flame, smoke and ashes to the accompaniment of the deafening noise of powerful hammers. But his greatest showpiece was the gigantic water wheel, regarded by many as the eighth wonder of the world; weighing one hundred tons, it used twenty-five tons of water a minute to power four massive furnaces, producing streams of molten metal. It was an awesome sight even for Nelson, who emerged from the inferno to be confronted by a great multitude, and like the Brecon farmers, Crawshay was overcome with emotion. With tears streaming down his cheeks he took Nelson by the arm, and turning to his men yelled 'shout you beggars', and they responded with a deafening roar that must have been heard on Dowlais top. One wonders just what it was about this charismatic little figure that moved strong men to tears, that engendered such love and loyalty in his brother officers, and made the ordinary seamen volunteer to serve with him time and time again, when they often preferred prison to serving on board other ships.

Rejoining the westward road at Trecastle, the tourists continued towards Carmarthen through Llandovery and

Llandeilo. Whether it was by accident or design, their night between Merthyr and Carmarthen was spent at Llandovery rather than Llandeilo. Could it have been that the travellers had read the comments of other tourists in Wales who had visited poor unfortunate Llandeilo? One, a Welshman to wit, observed 'As a town it is deserving of very little notice; the inn bad, the streets, if streets they be called, which streets are none, dirty, narrow and irregular.' So they stayed at Llandovery's Castle Inn where, before leaving for Carmarthen on the following day, Nelson signed a portrait for the landlord. From here, they continued on a pleasant drive through the beautiful Vale of Towy, taking them past that elevated ground at Llanarthney where, in a few short years, Sir William Paxton would erect his turreted folly, dedicated to the memory of Lord Nelson, the Hero of Trafalgar. It is a triangular stone tower with three entrances over which are inscribed in Welsh, English and Latin:

To the Invincible Commander, Viscount Nelson, in Com-memoration of Deeds before the Walls of Copenhagen, and on the Shores of Spain; of the Empire everywhere maintained by him over the seas; and of the death which in the fulness of his own glory, though ultimately for his own Country and for Europe, conquering, he died. This tower was erected by William Paxton.'

Time took its toll of this noble edifice, which fell into a deplorable state of disrepair, until a few years ago when it was adopted by the National Trust and it has since been restored to its former glory.

They were now in the land of Merlin, a land steeped in the old traditions of Celtic culture. Welsh was still the first language of the people – the hard-working farmers, the intriguing ladies in their native costumes with tall black hats, and the coracle fisherman silently harvesting the waters of the River Towy.

The party arrived in Carmarthen unaware that some civic

*The coracle fishermen were a familiar sight on Welsh rivers. Courtesy: Swansea City Library.*

*A west Wales Oysterwoman selling her wares – Nelson was a ready customer and bought some oysters for two shillings and sixpence. Courtesy: Swansea City Library.*

dignitaries were at odds as to whether or not they should receive Lady Hamilton, and it looked for a while as though there could be a repetition of the Blenheim incident. But things seemed to settle down following the resignation from the reception committee of the Vicar of Carmarthen, the Rev. William Higgs-Barker, who stated publicly 'I cannot wait upon Lady Hamilton, although to Lord Nelson personally I would cheerfully pay every respect', which seems to have been an appalling example of double standards for a man of the church. Perhaps he had read with some concern the comments of one contemporary writer who had observed: 'In point of population, Carmarthen is the fourth town in Wales. The trade of the place is considerable, but there is no internal manufacture to employ the poor who are very numerous, very burdensome to the inhabitants, and very profligate. I have been assured that the state of morals is more relaxed in this capital of South Wales than in any other part of the Principality. We may be permitted to hope that it has not been called Little London on this account!'

There was however, little prospect of the boisterous Lady Hamilton allowing a pious parson to cramp her style in West Wales, for she intended to be the hub of the visiting notabilities around which everything and everyone else would revolve. Besides, there were the dresses bought at Oxford to be shown off to the best advantage, which she intended to do one evening in front of a lively audience at the Playhouse Theatre where the veteran actor manager Henry Masterman put on a special performance for the occasion.[36] Nelson does not record in his accounts the payment of ten guineas he is supposed to have made to Masterman, but does note that he presented a guinea to a ventriloquist, probably the popular comic and impersonator Charles Matthews.

Despite a marked lack of inclination on the part of a few strict moralists to offer them the traditional warmth of Welsh hospitality, the visitors were obviously quite taken with Carmarthen, for they decided to stay in the town for two nights rather than one. But this may have been a last minute decision, since for some reason, they changed inns; having stayed the first night at the 'Ivy Bush', the second night was spent at the 'Three Tuns' in Bridge Street. They left before breakfast on the day of their departure, and reports have it that they went without any of the customary civic formalities, which so displeased Lord Nelson that he observed that 'there is not a gentleman in the place.'[37] Yet the pompous postures of civic and ecclesiastical big wigs rarely reflected the true feelings of the people, and we can be sure that the ordinary folk of Carmarthen, as in all the other towns and villages along the way, left their hero and his friends in no doubt of their loyal affection.

The ten miles of notoriously bad West Wales road which lay between Carmarthen and St. Clears were covered in time to breakfast at the Blue Boar Inn. Then it was on through a merry peel of bells at Narberth – where the ringers received a guinea for their exertions – through Haverfordwest, to a tumultuous flag-waving reception at Milford. It was late in the day when the two dusty carriages turned into Front Street, driving past buildings in every state of construction before coming to rest outside the New Inn, where Sir William's nephew Charles Greville, anxiously awaited their arrival.

# FOUR

MILFORD HAVEN – PICTON CASTLE – HAVERFORDWEST
– RIDGEWAY – STACKPOLE – TENBY – SWANSEA –
MARGAM – CARDIFF – NEWPORT

The following day was the glorious 1st August, and the town was dressed over-all to celebrate the fourth anniversary of Nelson's great triumph on the Nile at Aboukir. The people of Milford were proud and honoured to have the victor of the battle among them to join in a hectic programme of celebrations scheduled to last several days and including a regatta, fair, cattle show and boat races, all masterminded by Greville to popularise the amenities of his new town.[38] It was an inspired piece of showmanship which greatly pleased Sir William, who had speculated a fortune on the success of the town's development, a fact that was now causing him serious financial stress, as he had earlier made clear in a letter to his nephew:

My visit to Milford last year convinced me of the propriety of all your operations there, and which may still operate in my favour during the short time I can expect to live, but must be attended with immense profit to my heirs hereafter. You are perfectly acquainted with the present state of my finances, and are giving me your advice and friendly aid to get me as soon as possible out of my difficulties. I saw enough when at Milford, that was I to take upon me the management of your plans there, I should rather do hurt than good, and you know that I gave a publick testimony at the dinner there that I should continue to give you the full power of acting for me after your having given such proofs of your ability.

This same letter also gave more than a hint of his growing dissatisfaction with his domestic situation, of Emma's excesses and the barely concealed intimacy of her relationship with Nelson, which he accepted with a saintly tolerance:

It is but reasonable after having fagged all my life, that my last days should pass off comfortably and quietly. Nothing at present disturbs me but my debts, and the nonsense I am obliged to submit to here to avoid coming to an explosion which wou'd be attended with many disagreeable effects, and would totally destroy the comfort of the best man and the best friend I have in the world. However, I am determined that my quiet shall not be disturbed let the nonsensicall world go on as it will.[39]

The visitors spent the next few days at the New Inn where a sumptuous banquet, which was attended by all the leading lights of Pembrokeshire society, was held in their honour. Charles Greville had set the stage for Nelson to make a blockbuster of a speech, which both he and Sir William were convinced would put Milford well and truly on the map. His lordship opened with a warm tribute to the popular local hero Captain Thomas Foley, of whom he said, '. . . there is not a braver man in the King's service.' Thomas Foley had been with Nelson in all his major campaigns including the Battle of the Nile and Copenhagen, and his Commander considered that he deserved to share in every honour and public recognition. 'He is not only a Welshman' said Nelson, 'but a native of Pembrokeshire!'[40]

It was a generous compliment to a friend and brother officer, and a reflection of his high regard for Foley, which was perhaps never more manifest than at the Battle of Copenhagen. Having sailed to the Baltic on board HMS *St. George*, Nelson preferred a lighter ship for the battle, and chose to transfer to HMS *Elephant*, under the command of Captain Foley. At the height of the battle, Sir Hyde Parker,

*The 'New Town' of Milford. The main thoroughfare of Front Street, runs up to St Katherine's Chapel above Greville's quay and warehouses (centre left). From a watercolour by John 'Warwick' Smith.*

*Courtesy: National Library of Wales.*

*Pembrokeshire's own hero, Captain Thomas Foley, who served with Nelson at the Battle of the Nile and at Copenhagen. Courtesy: Dyfed County Library, Haverfordwest.*

thinking that Nelson was in trouble, signalled for him to discontinue the engagement. It was at this point that the now famous incident occurred when Nelson, putting the telescope to his blind eye remarked: 'You know Foley, I have only one eye, and I have a right to be blind sometimes. I really did not see the signal.' It was a perfect after-dinner story that would have gone down well with Nelson's Pembrokeshire audience. After the battle, he wrote – 'To Captain Foley, who permitted me the honour of hoisting my flag in the 'Elephant', I feel under the greatest obligations. His advice was necessary on many and important occasions during the battle.' Nelson would seek and earn even greater glory at sea, but for Foley, Copenhagen was the end of his sea-going career. In 1811, he was promoted to the rank of Rear Admiral and appointed Commander-in-Chief of the Downs with headquarters at Deal, where he remained until 1814. He was made a Knight Commander of the Bath, and in 1830, became Commander-in-Chief, Portsmouth, where he remained until his death in 1833.

Having spoken in the most generous terms of a Pembrokeshire man, Nelson went on at considerable length to extol the virtues of Milford, comparing it favourably with Trincomalee in the East Indies, then considered the best harbour in the world. To emphasize his point, he drew the attention of his listeners to the strategic importance of Milford, which 'Standing as it does between the Bristol and St. George's channels, makes it the only safe seaport on the west coast of Britain, for commercial as well as refuge and call. When viewed in relation to Ireland, it became the central port of the Empire, particularly as a bonding port.' He was full of praise for Lord Spencer's wisdom in promoting naval architecture at Milford, with its easy access to abundant ship-building timber on the banks of the River Severn. He was impressed too, with the quality of ships in the dockyard, built on the draughts of the talented French refugee shipbuilder, Jean-Louis Barrallier, which he considered models of their class in the British Navy. In conclusion, he told his audience that the port of Milford was now well-adapted to be of prime importance to Great Britain both commercially, and strategically to the navy. 'If only the Government would continue to give fair encouragement to the officers and seamen of the County of Pembrokeshire, it could not fail to render important service to the Nation.'[41] It was what today would be called a 'keynote' speech, clearly intended for a much wider and more influential audience, and if it reflected Nelson's own admiration for this fine neglected port, it also expressed Greville's desire for its commercial success.

Nelson's plea for government help was perhaps an indication of his impatience and concern at the tardiness of officialdom in adopting his suggestions, and the way in which it did so when the bureaucratic wheels eventually ground into motion. Indeed, he had personal experience of this after he lost the sight of an eye in action at Calvi. When, on returning to London, he went to the Pensions Office to receive a year's pay (the Navy's usual allowance for losing an eye or a limb), he was refused payment because he failed to produce a medical certificate testifying that the sight was in fact extinguished. Annoyed at what he considered a superfluous if not impertinent request, the loss being sufficiently notorious, he not only obtained a certificate for the eye, but also one for the missing arm, which was equally apparent – scathingly remarking: 'I might as well be doubted for one as well as the other.' When he eventually went to receive the sum due, which was the annual pay for a captain, (his rank at the time of his injuries), the clerk expressed the opinion that he thought it should perhaps have been more. 'Oh no' replied the admiral cynically, 'this is only for an eye; in a few days I shall return for an arm, and in a little time longer, God knows most probably for a leg.'

Greville beamed with pride and self-satisfaction as Nelson paid a special tribute to the town's generous benefactor, expressing his admiration of Sir William's plans, which had brought new opportunities to Milford: '. . . under

Picton Castle in Pembrokeshire, where Nelson and the Hamiltons were the guests of Lord Milford. Courtesy: Dyfed County Library, Haverfordwest.

*Stackpole Court, where Nelson and his party stayed with Lord Cawdor, who probably gave the admiral a firsthand account of the abortive attempt by the French to invade Pembrokeshire. Courtesy: Dyfed County Library, Haverfordwest.*

the judicious arrangements and unremitting perseverence of the Hon. Charles Greville.' Sir William completed the festivities with the presentation to the New Inn of an impressive full-length portrait of his renowned friend by the Palermo artist, Guzzardi.[42] The painting hung in the main room of the inn, later renamed the Lord Nelson, until 1847, when it was purchased for the boardroom of the Admiralty, where it now hangs. For posterity, Nelson scratched his name on a bedroom window pane, but unlike the portrait this has not survived.

It is perhaps surprising that neither Nelson, the erudite Sir William, nor Greville with his strong Warwickshire connections, quoted the words of Shakespeare to endorse their view of Milford Haven:

Tell me how Wales was made so happy as to inherit such a Haven!

Work on the new church planned by Greville had been speeded up to enable his uncle to lay the foundation stone during this visit. Dedicated to St. Katherine, the church was perhaps Sir William's memorial to his first wife, Katherine, who now lay buried at nearby Slebech. For many years the porch of the church housed the truck of the mainmast from the ill-fated French flagship *L'Orient*, retrieved from the sea by Sir Samuel Hood of H.M.S. *Zealous* whilst searching for survivors at the Battle of the Nile. Nelson's friend, Captain Benjamin Hallowel, Commander of H.M.S. *Swiftsure*, got his carpenter to make a coffin from the timber of the mainmast, using its metalwork to add some decoration to this macabre souvenir. He sent the coffin to Nelson with the hopeful message that '. . . the time is far distant when you may consider being buried in one of your own trophies.'[43]

From here the party went on a jaunt through the county, calling at the homes of the local gentry and aristocracy along the way. They were taken by boat up the inner waterways of the Haven to the waterside castle of Lord Milford at Picton, which is perhaps unique among historic mansions, having been inhabited by the lords of that place since the time of William Rufus. To come here was something of a pilgrimage for Sir William, for it was adjacent to the vast Slebech estate of the Barlow family, home of the first Lady Hamilton. She was a cultured though delicate woman who died of a fever in Naples in 1782, and in accordance with her wishes her body was brought back to Pembrokeshire to rest in the vault of the little chapel at Slebech, in the care of the Knights of St. John of Jerusalem.

The short stay at Picton gave Nelson and his friends an opportunity to explore some of the surrounding country-side, and although it was early August, they bought some of the wares of a local oysterman which, Nelson noted, cost them two shillings and sixpence. Although Nelson refers to an 'Oyster Man', one wonders if perhaps the trippers were not taken in by the appearance of the 'Ladies of Llangwm'. Of almost pure Flemish stock, these robust women dressed in men's wide brimmed hats and trousers, with panniers over their broad backs to peddle the succulent oysters for which Llangwm had for centuries been famous.[44]

On leaving Picton, the party proceeded to Haverfordwest, where they were enthusiastically greeted by clamouring crowds who took the horses from the carriages, which they then drew with an escort of Lord Milford's Yeomanry, to Foley House in Goat Street, where the visitors stayed overnight. On Saturday 7 August, a meeting of the Common Council unanimously passed a resolution proposed by Lord Milford, conferring the full freedom of the Town and County of Haverfordwest on Horatio, Viscount Nelson, and his brother officer, Captain Thomas Foley. It was all done in something of a hurry, and having passed the resolution, Mayor Robert Batemen-Prust hastened with the Corporation to Foley House, where scrolls were presented to the new freemen as the Royal Pembrokeshire Militia Band played patriotic airs.[45]

From Haverfordwest, they travelled some eight miles to the elegant mansion of John Foley, brother of Captain Foley

*Slebech Hall on the Barlow estate; in the foreground the little chapel where Sir William Hamilton and his first wife Katherine lie together in the vault. Courtesy: Dyfed County Library, Haverfordwest.*

*Ridgeway, where Nelson and the Hamiltons were the guests of Captain Foley's brother John. From an original drawing by Haydn Barrington.*

who now accompanied the party. The Nash-style house was approached along a drive, brightly lit with hundreds of lanterns and flickering candles to welcome the celebrated guests. Surprisingly perhaps, another potentially embarrassing situation seemed in prospect when John Foley's wife expressed misgivings about entertaining Lady Hamilton in her home. She was, however, persuaded to put aside her inhibitions and enter into the spirit of the occasion, if only for the sake of her brother-in-law Thomas, who had just returned from London with a new bride.[46] There was an extravagant dinner, after which Emma may well have entertained the company with a song, or even a performance of her 'classical attitudes'; and although it was well past bedtime, the Foley's six-year old daughter Emily, was allowed down to meet the guests. She is said to have been a little unsure at first of the gentleman with only one arm and a patch over his eye, but her anxiety was quickly dispelled when the kindly figure hoisted her onto his knee and kept her amused by dropping grapes into her open mouth. As he did so, his thoughts and the thoughts of Emma, may well have strayed back to Merton and their own little daughter Horatia, who had been left in the care of her maternal grandmother.

Having spent two blissfully relaxing days with their friends, they left Ridgeway on 10 August, travelling south of Pembroke to Stackpole Court, home of Lord and Lady Cawdor, which was their last port of call before starting for home. The original mansion, constructed of locally quarried black marble, was situated on an estate with lakes covering an area of more than eighty acres, abundant in water lilies and lazing pike. It was a romantic and serenely beautiful setting, and the visitors must have regretted that their stay was so brief. Perhaps Sir William also lamented that time would not permit him to pit his angling skills against the pike. Fleeting though this visit was, it is probable that Nelson listened with rapt attention to Lord Cawdor's first-hand account of the French invasion of Pembrokeshire just five years before, perhaps even wishing he had been there himself to repel his old enemy. After less than twenty-four hours at Stackpole, they moved on to Tenby, unaware that within a few months, one of their number would return to the county for the last time, to lie for ever beside his devoted first wife in a vault at Slebech.

Ships of the King's Navy which were anchored offshore and dressed over-all, fired a deafening salute as Nelson entered the historic walled town of Tenby.[47] Yet again, his carriage was engulfed by an excited populace eager to take over the task of the horses. Perhaps by now he was feeling the effects of the long days and late nights of Pembrokeshire hospitality, for one onlooker observed that he looked far from well. In the early nineteenth century, the fashionable seaside town of Tenby was a favourite resort of the upper echelons of society and a visit from the great Lord Nelson was bound to enhance its reputation; but there was one crusty old visitor who was clearly out of step with popular feeling concerning the Admiral's visit, and in a letter he recorded his impressions of what he saw:

> I was yesterday witness to an exhibition which though greatly ridiculous, was not wholly so, for it was likewise pitiable; and this was in the persons of two individuals who have lately occupied much public attention. I mean the Duke of Bronte, Lord Nelson, and Emma, Lady Hamilton. The whole town was at their heels as they walked together. The lady is grown immensely fat and equally coarse, while her 'companion in arms' had taken the other extreme – thin, shrunken and to my impression in bad health. They were evidently vain of each other as though the one would have said 'This is Horatio of the Nile' and the other 'This is Emma of Sir William'. Poor Sir William, wretched but not abashed; he followed at a short distance bearing in his arms a cucciolo (small dog) and other emblems of their combined folly.[48]

The style and sentiments could be mistaken for Nelson's old friend Lord Minto, but in fact the trio were the butt of a certain Mr. Gore, who was apparently on holiday in the town. He was clearly out to find fault, for his impressions of the local theatre were equally uncomplimentary: 'Truly it is no bigger than a bulky bathing machine, and bears the same proportions to Sadlers Wells as a silver penny to a Spanish dollar.'[49] But an intimate theatre with strolling players obviously suited Nelson and his friends, for our critical chronicler goes on to record – 'They play the Mock Doctor tonight and the Hero of the Nile is the subject of an address.' On the following night the party dined with Lord Kensington, and afterwards attended a Grand Ball at the Lion Inn, to bring the hectic social round in Pembrokeshire to an end. They had all enjoyed Tenby, and Nelson expressed himself particularly pleased with the marine prospect of the place.

Everyone agreed that the visit to Pembrokeshire had been an outstanding success which, it could be fairly claimed, had taken the county by storm, and would be remembered for generations to come. It was now time to embark on the long homeward trek, taking them back through St. Clears to Carmarthen, where the local populace towed the carriages to the 'Kings Arms'; but this time they stayed only long enough to take on fresh horses to carry them to their next port of call – Swansea.

In 1802, Swansea was an important and expanding seafaring town with a population of almost seven thousand, justifiably claiming to be second only to Merthyr Tydfil in size and importance in the Principality. The writer Malkin considered it to be the cleanest town in Wales, '. . . where the streets are everywhere swept clean early in the morning, and strewed with sand.' They arrived here on 13 August, and were met at Fforestfach by what the *Cambrian* afterwards described as a '. . . . choice body of tars exulting in the happiness and glory they had, in showing their respects to one of their own body – the Hero of the Age and Restorer of Peace and Plenty.' In the now familiar way, the carriages were unhorsed to be hauled into the town through hoards of cheering people. The berobed portreeve met the visitors at the turnpike gates and escorted a good-natured procession to Wind Street, where the shouting reached a crescendo as milling crowds threatened to engulf the carriages.

At that time, there lived in Swansea a retired seaman by the name of Tom Cleaves, who had been a boatswain on one of Nelson's ships. He was now the licensee of 'The Plume of Feathers', and also a bell-ringer at the parish church. But today he had good reason for deserting the belfry to join the crowds in Wind Street. While his fellow campanologists peeled out their joyful welcome to the nation's hero, Cleaves jostled and elbowed his way through a sea of bodies to a position near the carriage carrying Nelson. Taking his old boatswain's pipe from his pocket he put it to his lips, and blew three high-pitched and very distinctive blasts. At this Nelson sprang from his seat, and scanning the crowd cried, 'It's Tom Cleaves' whistle by God.' The carriages were immediately ordered to stop, and the people of Swansea witnessed an emotional reunion between the Admiral and the veteran bosun. It is likely that Cleaves drew Nelson's attention to the strenuous efforts of the friends he had left in the belfry, for Nelson sent them a present of two guineas.

The visitors were joined by Sir William's friend, the influential Swansea industrialist Mr. John Morris, whose guests they would be for dinner at his Clasemont home. On the drive up to Clasemont, the carriages stopped at the Mackworth Arms so that the landlord, Mr. Roteley (a particular friend of Morris) and his teenage son Lewis, who was keen to join the navy, might meet the admiral. The lad idolised Nelson, who quizzed him on his knowledge of the sea and ships, and young Lewis so impressed his hero that he was given a letter of introduction to the Cadet Training School at Portsmouth, recommending him for enrolment as a trainee seaman.[51]

The young Swansea boy was not to know that little more than three years hence he would, as a marine officer, share in the glory of Trafalgar, and witness the death of his hero

42

*A mid nineteenth-century view of Wind Street, scene of Nelson's reunion with his old bosun, Tom Cleaves. On the extreme left is the Mackworth Arms, home of the young marine officer, Lewis Roteley.*
*Courtesy: Swansea City Library.*

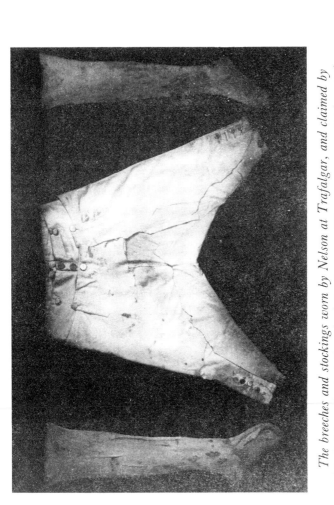

The breeches and stockings worn by Nelson at Trafalgar, and claimed by Lt. Roteley who took them back to Swansea. They are now on display at the National Maritime Museum, Greenwich. Courtesy: Trustees, The National Maritime Museum.

below the decks of H.M.S. *Victory*.[52] Years later, after returning home to Swansea following an active life at sea, he related his eye-witness account of the tragic moment when Nelson fell.

> I saw the mizzen top of the French ship 'Redoubtable' crowded with marines, and realised they were intent on firing at a particular part of 'Victory's' deck. Seeing their design, I ordered my men to send some volleys into their midst, but alas, we were too late to prevent the fatal shot and I saw, to my horror, Lord Nelson fall on the deck with blood oozing from his breast.

Nelson was taken below decks where he died of his wounds. When the battle was over, the young marine officer seeing Nelson's blood-stained breeches and stockings in a corner, requested permission to take them, and was allowed to do so. He took the precious relics back to his native Swansea, where they remained in his family's possession until 1896 when, on the death of Miss Jean Rotely, they were bequeathed to the Royal Hospital at Greenwich and are now on permanent exhibition at the National Maritime Museum.[53]

On 14 August, the portreeve gave a banquet to commemorate this memorable visit at which the freedom of the borough was conferred on both Lord Nelson and Sir William Hamilton. Not to be eclipsed by the menfolk, Lady Hamilton aroused the patriotic zeal of all those present by bringing the proceeding to a close with a spirited rendering of *Rule Britannia*.

It is probable that on Sunday 15 August the whole party attended the parish church, for Nelson was the devout son of a country parson, and brother of the clergyman William. They certainly inspected the town's pier and harbour, and were shown over the famous Coles and Haynes Pottery.[54] The owners had recently installed hot and cold sea water baths on their premises and for one shilling and three pence, patrons could have a cold bath with a fire in the dressing room, or the additional luxury of a hot bath with a fire for three shillings. Customers could also enjoy '. . . in the strictest privacy, the exhilarating effects of sea bathing under cover, and with the aid of bathing machines erected entirely in the Italian plan.' Italian bathing machines must surely have earned the approval of Sir William and Emma, perhaps rekindling fond memories of warmer Neapolitan shores. The visitors are said to have taken advantage of this unusual opportunity to refresh themselves, before continuing the excursion on dusty roads at the height of summer to the eastern side of Swansea Bay and the superbly sited residence of Thomas Mansel Talbot at Margam. Did Sir William, one wonders, echo the thoughts of that frequent visitor to the area, Walter Savage Landor, who likened Swansea Bay to the Bay of Naples? Had he possessed the energy and the inclination to climb the heights above Margam, he could not have failed to make the comparison for himself, as might anyone who has surveyed the magnificent Bay of Naples from the summit of Vesuvius.

Passing through Aberavon on his way to Margam, Nelson sent a message saying that he would like to pay his respects to the portreeve. The portreeve was, however, quite unprepared for this unexpected honour, as he was at the time repairing the roof of a neighbour's house. Not wishing to appear neglectful of his civic duties or wanting to miss the opportunity of paying homage to such an illustrious caller, he quickly changed into his best clothes and hurried off to meet the great man. After fulfilling his obligations the official, with due dignity, escorted the important visitor to his carriage. As he bowed and doffed his hat to take his leave of Nelson, he stammered the hope that his lordship would please remember the portreeve. The admiral could no longer suppress his amusement at the manner of his reception, and promised: 'I will remember you. By God I shall never forget you, to the last day of my life.'[55]

Mansel Talbot's exotic gardens at Margam could boast one of the finest collections of trees in the country,

*Sir William Hamilton's friend John Morris, Swansea industrialist, from whom the district of Morriston takes its name. Courtesy: Swansea City Library.*

*Thomas Horner's painting of the Chapter House Ruins and the Orangery at Margam. It was built by Thomas Mansel Talbot to house his collection of exotic orange and lemon trees. Courtesy: Swansea City Library.*

including an enormous Aleppo pine with a girth measuring more than eleven feet.[56] The owner of Margam was himself the wealthy son of a Wiltshire parson and had probably met Sir William at Naples, when doing the 'Grand Tour' in 1770. If, however, the former ambassador had hoped to become re-acquainted with a kindred spirit, he was to be disappointed, for having arrived at Margam without giving prior notice, the visitors were informed that Mr. Talbot was not at home. So it was left to the head gardener to conduct the distinguished callers through the grounds and show them Talbot's splendid orangery, a masterpiece of eighteenth century classical architecture measuring three hundred and twenty-seven feet in length.[57] Originally built to house its proud owner's famous collection of orange trees and several new varieties of citrus trees, it later fell into a deplorable state of decay and was in need of urgent and extensive repairs when it was acquired by the West Glamorgan County Council in 1973. After careful renovation by its new owners, it was eventually restored to its former grandeur and must now rank as one of the finest pieces of classical architecture in the whole of Wales.

In common with Sir William, Mansel Talbot was an art connoisseur and an avid collector who brought back to this country many of Italy's antiquities, including a fine collection of statues despatched from Leghorn to Swansea by sea. These were on display in the orangery and grounds of Margam, a circumstance which must have made the visit a particularly pleasurable experience for the retired diplomat. It was a gratifying day too for the head gardener, for not only had he conducted Britain's most celebrated naval hero around the park, but had received from him the princely sum of three shillings for doing so. Even though this sum included a generous tip, had they not paid the gardener it is doubtful whether even the great Lord Nelson would have been allowed into the park, since charging visitors for admittance was one of his 'perks', and all visitors were expected to pay.

Whilst at Margam, Nelson visited Dr. William Llewellyn, who had retired from the navy due to ill-health and settled at Margam where he established himself as the parish's first resident doctor. On leaving there, they continued at a leisurely pace through the pastoral Vale of Glamorgan, stopping only to change horses and refresh themselves at the Pyle Inn and at Cowbridge. The bill of £7.15s. 9d. does, however, suggest that they stayed overnight at Cardiff, but other than this brief mention in Nelson's own accounts, no other record of his stay here seems to exist. Perhaps this is not surprising since there were still no newspapers in that part of Wales, and with a population of less than two thousand, Cardiff was a place of little importance with no pretensions to becoming the Principality's capital city. From Cardiff they proceeded to Newport, crossing the muddy estuary of the River Usk, to continue on the road to the border town of Chepstow, fifteen miles away on the banks of the Wye.

*Cardiff viewed from the west bank of the River Taff. Painted by Thomas Horner in 1819. Courtesy: Swansea City Library.*

*Nineteenth-century sailing ships berthed on the River Usk at Newport. Courtesy: Monmouth Museum.*

# FIVE

CHEPSTOW – MONMOUTH – RUDHALL – HEREFORD –
LEOMINSTER – LUDLOW – DOWNTON – PENCOMBE –
TENBURY WELLS – WORCESTER

At Chepstow the travellers put up at a small inn known as
the 'Three Cranes' just off the town's Beaufort Square. The
former inn is now a private house bearing the name
'St.Maur' and on the front a bronze plaque mounted on oak
from Nelson's flagship, *Victory*, commemorates the visit:

> In this house, then the 'Three Cranes', Horatio Nelson and
> party stayed 17th–18th August, 1802.[58]

An amusing incident occurred while Nelson and his
friends were dining there on the evening of their arrival. A
message was brought to him from a man outside claiming to
be a former sailor, who wished to pay his respects to his
former commander. The caring admiral responded by sending the man a bowl of soup, to which the servant was about
to add a spoon. 'Nay', said Nelson, 'by this token I shall
know whether or not he be one of my tars.' The soup was
taken out to the seaman by the servant who expected to see
him drink it up but, to everyone's surprise and amusement,
the old salt took from his pocket a small box containing
tobacco which he emptied of its contents, then used it as a
spoon. Nelson was told of this peculiar ritual, immediately
recognised the man as one of his own sailors, and gave him a
few shillings to 'splice the mainbrace'.

Before resuming their journey on the following day, the
tourists walked through the town to view the historic castle

47

and admire its challenging situation high on the rocks at the mouth of the Wye. After leaving Chepstow, they had progressed little more than a mile on the road to Monmouth, when they turned into Piercefield Park, now the site of Chepstow racecourse. It was at that time the home of Mr. and Mrs. Nathaniel Wells, and the gardens overlooking the river were a showpiece without equal anywhere in the county. The gardens were cleverly landscaped to incorporate woodland walks and grottos above perpendicular cliffs rising several hundred feet above the river in the valley below. Viewing platforms with seats enabled visitors to admire the dramatic views of the Wye estuary and the River Severn beyond in leisurely comfort. Each viewing point was given a name to indicate what visitors might expect to see; there was 'Grotto', 'Alcove', 'Double View', 'Druid's Temple', 'Giant's Cave', and one wonders if Emma and her dear Nelson mused awhile at 'Lovers' Leap'. Within these grounds stood Piercefield House, an imposing stone mansion, now sadly little more than a shell.

To get to Monmouth from Piercefield, tourists could take either one of two routes, the most direct being little more than a footpath along the riverbank, which would have taken them to the objective of most Wye Valley visitors, the historic ruin of Tintern Abbey. The alternative was a charming route on a rough carriage road from St. Arvans, over Wyndcliff and through Devauden to Trelech, from whence they could drive down to Monmouth.

In those days, the Wye was a busy navigable river on whose banks a wide variety of trades flourished, served by the barges and trows that crossed the Severn to Bristol.[59] There, at the Welsh Back, the historic inn known as the 'Llandoger Trow' still stands to remind us of this once prosperous trading link. Had Nelson and his party taken the riverside route to Monmouth, they might have witnessed the extraordinary sight of teams of men, harnessed to tow ropes, heaving the flat-bottomed barges upstream. It took five muscular men to pull an empty barge – fifteen when it

*The great border
castle at Chepstow,
admired by Nelson
and his friends as
they walked
through the town
viewing places of
interest. Drawn by
T. Hearne FSA,
1798. Courtesy:
Chepstow Museum.*

Piersfield House, Chepstow, where Nelson and the Hamiltons were entertained by Mr and Mrs Nathaniel Wells. From an early nineteenth-century drawing by G. Eyre Brooks. Courtesy: Chepstow Museum.

was fully laden – for a barge weighed twenty-five tons or more. Negotiating the weirs demanded the most strenuous exertions, as the men fell face down with all their weight on the ground; then to the shout of 'Yo ho' they strained to hold their ground, before rising up at another shout to advance one more step. Would Nelson, one wonders, have agreed with that tireless chronicler Charles Heath, who considered it to be work that '. . . none but British hearts would have the courage to call forth and persevere in. A frog eating Frenchman and more idle Spaniard would be drowned in the attempt!'

Heath also records a more agreeable meaning for the term 'mugging':

A curious custom between the owners and watermen, prevails at all the ports on the River Severn, but only at Monmouth on the Wye. Every man when hired for a voyage receives a pint of ale as earnest of his services – which is called 'mugging' – and if he does not fulfil the stipulated labour, he is liable to three months in prison. Also, if the master afterwards refuses to employ the bargeman, the servant has the power to demand wages from him as though he had performed the voyage. Hence, when a man is a little – 'how came you so?' – we say he has been 'mugging' himself.

Today, many visitors to Monmouth are curious to know of the town's special connection with Nelson, and why it has such a fine collection of memorabilia in the Nelson Museum. It is probably true to say that Monmouth is particularly indebted to three factors – two people, and a unique memorial – for the preservation of its association with the admiral. The first person is Charles Heath, who was a printer, bookseller and a prolific writer on local history and topography at the time of Nelson's visit. He recorded for posterity the gossipy accounts of Nelson's presence in the town, including the speeches and private conversations that took place between himself and the distinguished visitors, and other townsfolk who were fortunate enough to meet

49

them. Heath committed it all to his powerful little printing press, and the valuable accounts that he published then have now become much sought-after collectors' pieces.

The other person to whom the town and its visitors are indebted is Georgiana, Lady Llangattock, mother of the pioneer aviator C.S. Rolls, who lived at 'The Hendre', a beautiful estate on the outskirts of Monmouth. Lady Llangattock was an avid collector of anything remotely connected with Nelson, including volumes of his correspondence. She bequeathed her collection, the most comprehensive outside the National Maritime Museum at Greenwich, to the town in 1924, and it is this which forms the nucleus of Monmouth Museum's Nelson Collection.

The unique memorial is the Naval Temple on the picturesque Kymin Hill overlooking the town, from where the visitor can enjoy a grand panorama of great beauty stretching from the Malvern Hills in the north, to the Brecon Beacons and beyond in the west. The temple was erected on the summit of this idyllic mound in 1800 as a memorial to the British Navy, and to those admirals who distinguished themselves in the naval battles of the latter part of the eighteenth century. On 18 August 1802, the most illustrious of those admirals paid his second visit to Monmouth, and the people were eager that he should grace this noble edifice with his presence.

True to the promise made to Mayor Hollings on the outward journey, Nelson dispatched a letter from St. Clears in Carmarthenshire, confirming his intention to pay a second visit to the town:

St. Clairs                                                    August 14th 1802

Sir,

You and several members of the Corporation wishing to know a few days previous to my return through Monmouth, I now beg leave to tell you that I shall be at Monmouth with our party on Thursday, to accept the honour of the polite invitation we have received. I am Sir, with much respect, your obliged friend.

T. Hollings Esq:                                          Nelson and Bronte[60]

*Lady Llangattock attending the centenary celebrations of the Battle of Trafalgar at the Naval Temple on 21st October 1905. Courtesy: Nelson Museum, Monmouth.*

*Lord and Lady Llangattock drive through crowds in Agincourt Square, Monmouth, to celebrate the centenary of Trafalgar in 1905. Courtesy: Nelson Museum, Monmouth.*

Loyal little Monmouth was *en fête* on the morning following Nelson's arrival. As the bells of St. Mary's Church proclaimed his presence in the town, he emerged from the Beaufort at 9 o'clock into Agincourt Square, which was swarming with people who occupied every vantage point to watch him drive in a carriage through the narrow streets teeming with cheering townsfolk, all the way to Wye Bridge. The carriage trundled over the old stone bridge and took the steep narrow track to the summit of the Kymin.[61] Like the Naval Temple, the Kymin Pavilion is now owned by the National Trust, and its origins are just as interesting. Its construction was ordered by a number of local gentlemen who met each year for a social outing to enjoy a pipe and a song with a cold collation at one of the local beauty spots. In 1793, the venue was the Kymin, and the outing proved to be so enjoyable that several more meetings on the hill were arranged during that summer. The preference for this location was firmly established and in the following year, the friends, who now styled themselves 'The Kymin Club', approved plans for a summer house to be erected at their own expense, where they could meet regularly whatever the state of the weather. At the end of two years a fine turreted tower standing thirty feet high with two rooms, one on the ground floor containing the kitchen, and a banqueting room upstairs which, to quote Heath, '. . . was fitted up in a manner suitable for the purposes of friendship and conviviality.' It was in this room that Nelson and his party sat down to breakfast with the mayor and corporation, before going on to inspect the Naval Temple, and the table reputedly used on this occasion is now in the Nelson Museum.

They walked the few yards from the Pavilion to the main object of their interest, the Naval Temple, surmounted by a seated figure of Britannia. On a frieze around its walls were sixteen medallions each bearing the name of one of the sixteen naval commanders in whose honour the monument had been erected, and the dates of the battles in which they

51

had distinguished themselves. A white marble tablet records:

> This Naval Temple was erected August 1st 1800 to perpetuate the names of those noble Admirals who distinguished themselves by their glorious victories for England in the last and present wars, and is respectfully dedicated to her grace the Duchess of Beaufort, daughter of Admiral Boscawen.

On the east wall was a dramatic painting depicting the Battle of the Nile, which Nelson scrutinised with a keen eye. The contemporary chronicler Heath, noted: 'As his Lordship proceeded round the temple, I felt a desire to witness the manner of his viewing the painting of his glorious victory, as well as the sensation it might create in his mind, for which purpose I took my station near him. On his Lordship's arrival at this part of the building, he surveyed with an opera glass, which he held in his hand, this representation of his fame, without the least emotion, as though it had been accomplished by another officer, and after pausing on it for some minutes, directed his attention to different objects around him.' With the sharp ear of a reporter, Heath eavesdropped on a snatch of the Admiral's conversation with Mr. Hardwick, on whose arm he was resting and to whom he acidly asserted: 'I hate the French', before going on to compliment him on the erection of the Temple, saying that it was not only one of the most beautiful places he had ever seen, but to the boast of Monmouth, it was the only monument of its kind erected to the English navy throughout the length and breadth of the kingdom. 'The Nation', he said, 'has been engaged for some time in collecting money in order to erect by public subscription a magnificent structure of this kind, without accomplishing its purpose. This at the Kymin is enough; and for which the Admirals whose services are here recorded are very much obliged to you.'

Now in the care of the National Trust, the Temple is

*An original oil painting by the Monmouth artist John Arthur Evans, showing the Naval Temple and the Pavilion on the Kymin where the celebrated visitors breakfasted. Courtesy: Monmouth Museum.*

*The ancient Buckstone – made to resemble a 'Welsh cottage without a chimney' when it was whitewashed for Nelson's visit. Courtesy: Monmouth Museum.*

undergoing the most extensive and faithful restoration. Once this is completed visitors will be able to see it exactly as it was in the summer of 1802.

After spending some time viewing the Naval Temple, Nelson turned his attention to nearby Beaulieu Grove, and the woods belonging to Lord Gage on the edge of the forest. 'Is there any navy timber among it?' he enquired of a bystander, who replied, 'It does indeed contain a very fine plank.' 'Aye', said his Lordship, 'plank is very useful,' displaying his ever-present concern for forestry and timber-production. On holiday he may have been, but even as he drifted lazily down the Wye towards Monmouth on that peaceful Sunday afternoon some weeks earlier, he was still observing and taking notes: 'The first thing necessary in the Forest of Dean is to plant some acres of acorns and I saw plenty of clear fields with cattle grazing in my voyage down the Wye in two years these will be fit for transplanting.' The bystander to whom Nelson addressed his remarks concerning the forest might well have been James Davies, an agent of Lord Gage, who wrote to his lordship:

How do you approve of Lord Nelson and Lady Hamilton travelling about the country as they do? I suppose on their accounts, the poor old Buckstone was whitewashed. They were expected to spend a day at the Kymin which they did, and great preparations were made by Mr. Hardwick, but he denies knowing anything of this mistaken ornament. It now looks like a small Welsh cottage without a chimney, and a deal of time and trouble has been bestowed upon it.'[62]

At about 2 o'clock the visitors descended the Kymin, returning to town on foot rather than by carriage, so that more people might have an opportunity to see the illustrious tar at close quarters. We can be sure that the whole town hummed with activity and excited anticipation as attention was once more focused on 'The Beaufort', where a grand civic banquet was being prepared in Nelson's honour.

Promptly at four o'clock the Admiral entered the room, elegantly dressed in a blue frock-coat with gold epaulets, a black silk waistcoat, knee breeches, and a glittering array of orders and decorations. He was ushered to the place of honour beside the Mayor, with Lady Hamilton on hand to assist in cutting his food which, with only one arm, he found somewhat difficult. It was the great moment that the little town of Monmouth had been waiting for, as the distinguished assembly sat down to a memorable feast which included venison sent across the Severn from the Duke of Beaufort's estate at Badminton.

The contemporary local chronicler Charles Heath takes up the story:

After the cloth had been removed, and the health of our gracious Sovereign, with that of the other branches of the Royal Family, remembered in our glasses, Mr. Hollings gave as a toast from the Chair,

'The Health Of Lord Nelson, with thanks to his Lordship for his most important Public Services.'

Soon as the toast was drank and the company were seated, his Lordship rose up, and in the most dignified and eloquent manner, (worthy of the Hero of the Nile and Copenhagen) commanding at once the profound attention and respect of all present, addressed the meeting in the following, never to be forgotten words.

'Gentlemen, I beg leave to return you my most respectful thanks, for the honour done me in drinking my health, and also for the acknowledgement of the important public services, you are pleased to say I have rendered my country. It was my good fortune to have under my command some of the most experienced officers in the English Navy, whose professional skill was seconded by the undaunted courage of British Sailors; and whatever merit might attach itself to me, I must declare, that I had only to show them the enemy, and Victory Crowned The Standard!

'The British Navy has received a large portion of public applause; but however well deserved, it should be told that the same valour and sense of duty would have marked the conduct of the British Army, had it been placed in such situations as would have afforded it an equal opportunity of displaying its national courage; but it has unluckily happened that the same good fortune, in this instance, did not occur, or we should have had equal reason for praising its heroism and public services.

'When the English Army was sent to Egypt, it was the opinion of many intelligent characters, that it would be destroyed. For my own part, I never thought so, – for wherever the British Soldiers have opposed those of France, they have uniformly conquered them.

'In my own person, I have received an overflowing measure of the Nation's gratitude, far more than I either merited or expected; because the same success would have crowned the efforts of any other British Admiral, who had under his command such distinguished officers and such gallant crews. And here let me impress it on the mind of every Officer in the service, – that to whatever quarter of the globe he may be destined; whether to the East or West Indies, to Africa or America, the eyes of his Country are upon him; and, so long as public men, in public stations, exert themselves in those situations, to fulfil the duty demanded from them by the public, they will always find the British Nation ready to heap upon them the utmost extent of its gratitude and its applause.!'

Mirth and song now began to hold their influence over the meeting; and immediately on his Lordship being seated, Lady Hamilton favoured the company with a song, in appropriate words to the National Air of God Save the King, with the highest effect.

The appropriate words referred to by Heath were contained in the popular additonal verse by the Hamiltons' friend, Miss Cornelia Knight —

> Join we great Nelson's name,
> First on the roll of fame,
> Him let us sing,
> Spread we his praise around,
> Honour of British ground,
> Who made Nile's shores resound,
> God Save the King.

55

Heath's account of the proceedings continues:

During the course of the evening, many other very excellent songs were given, particularly by Mr. Callendar and Mr. Yarworth, which were received with great marks of approbation; – and, after the song of the British Grenadiers, by the Hon. John Lindsay, Lord Nelson again rose up; and, in his former dignified and impressive manner, addressed the meeting in the following words.

'Gentlemen, I must repeat my obligations to you, for the marked attentions I have received from the inhabitants of Monmouth, as well as from the company assembled on the present occasion. Nor can I leave you without wishing to impress my sentiments on your minds, and to bring them home to the feelings of every individual.

'Whenever the British Army has been opposed to French forces, without the incumbrance of German, Russian or other auxiliaries, it has invariably defeated them. The fact is, all the great battles the French obtained were over our allies, and not over the British Soldiers; and if those allies had been as faithful to the engagements as ourselves, the French would not have to boast of what they deem 'their splendid victories'.

'Gentlemen, I shall now speak to you as an Englishman; if war was again to take place, I would send every ship, every regular soldier, out the kingdom and leave the nation to be protected entirely by the courage of her sons at home. I remember in 1759, there were great threats of a French invasion! – but all reasonable men only smiled at the idea of such an attempt. Suppose the French were to land in England, what would be the consequence? They might plunder and destroy a village, – they might burn Monmouth, – but I will engage for it they never would advance as far as Hereford, for they would always find Britons ready to receive them. In all the histories of Kingdoms and States that I have read, it was the want of unanimity among themselves that produced their fall, and that alone will be able to effect the overthrow of our own. For so long as the people continue to unite Hand and Heart (as we have seen on the late threatened invasion by the French) we have nothing to fear, either from their efforts, or from those of all the world united in arms against us!'

56

*A portrait of Lady Hamilton wearing the Maltese Cross, painted by Schmidt, at Dresden in 1800. She was awarded the decoration in recognition of her service in securing supplies for Malta during the French occupation in 1798. It was Nelson's favourite portrait of Emma, and hung in his quarters on HMS Victory. Courtesy: Trustees, The National Maritime Museum.*

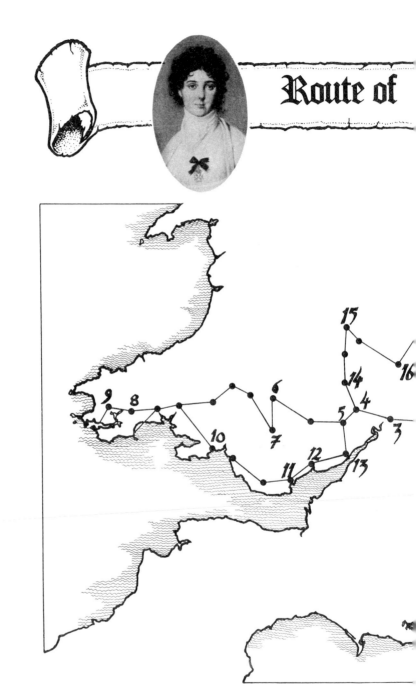

Route of

# the Tour

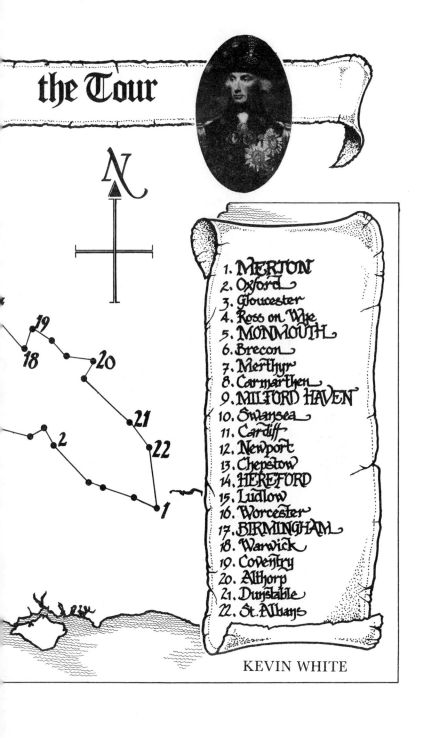

N

1. MERTON
2. Oxford
3. Gloucester
4. Ross on Wye
5. MONMOUTH
6. Brecon
7. Merthyr
8. Carmarthen
9. MILFORD HAVEN
10. Swansea
11. Cardiff
12. Newport
13. Chepstow
14. HEREFORD
15. Ludlow
16. Worcester
17. BIRMINGHAM
18. Warwick
19. Coventry
20. Althorp
21. Dunstable
22. St. Albans

KEVIN WHITE

*Portrait by L.F. Abbott of Lord Nelson wearing the
Plume of Triumph received from the Sultan of Turkey
for saving the Turkish province of Egypt from the
French. Courtesy: Trustees, The National Maritime
Museum.*

It was an inspiring performance, one that those who lived through the second world war might well compare with Churchill's speeches of the dark and seemingly hopeless days of the 1940s when Britain stood alone: 'Should the invader come to Britain, there will be no placid lying down of the people in submission as we have seen, alas, in other countries. We shall defend every village, every town, and every city. The vast mass of London itself fought street by street, could easily devour an entire hostile army.' Here is the proof, if proof is needed, that the spirit of Britain does not die with her heroes, but is passed on like a torch from generation to generation!

Heath continues: 'At the conclusion of Nelson's second address, Lady Hamilton sung appropriate words to the national air Rule Britannia, with such taste and powers of execution, as called forth the utmost astonishment and delight in the mind of every person at table. The talents indeed, of those professional British females the writer heard at the London theatres, were placed at an immeasurable distance, when compared with the vocal accomplishments of this Lady.'

Heath was probably unaware that Emma had been trained in Naples by the renowned Giuseppe Aprile, under whose masterly tuition she had developed into a fine coloratura soprano. Sir William proudly boasted to his friends of her fluency in Italian and French, and how, with her singing, she had surprised the very best of Naples' music masters. It is said that she was offered a contract to sing at La Scala for a fee of £2000 a year.

During the table-talk, Mr. Henry Parry seized the opportunity to question Nelson about his most recent battle off Copenhagen. 'It has been ascerted my Lord, that the action of that day was more severely contested than the Battle of the Nile.' 'Yes Sir', replied the Admiral. 'If that had been a French fleet, I should have destroyed them in two hours; but the Danes fought like men!' Nelson was never slow to voice his contempt of the French!

At eight o'clock on this warm August evening, the guests adjourned to the home of one Colonel Lindsay, in Monnow Street, where they relaxed over coffee in the garden summer-house. Heath summed up the evening in his customary colourful way: 'Never were the feast of reason and the flow of soul more happily enjoyed than at this meeting. His Lordship addressed the company with an energy peculiarly his own, – whose words like the notes of her ladyship, might be said still to vibrate on our ears; and I may venture to assert, there is not a person who shared in its pleasures that would, for a very large boon, dismiss the recollection of them from his memory.'

On the following day, Nelson and his party enjoyed themselves like countless other tourists by taking a leisurely stroll through the town to view its many objects of interest, still with a large flock of admirers following closely at their heels. In Agincourt Square they wandered into Charles Heath's book shop, to be greeted by a beaming proprietor who was soon busily chatting with his celebrated callers. 'Did not Lord Nelson speak well to you yesterday Mr. Heath?' enquired Lady Hamilton. 'And did not your Ladyship sing well to us', was Heath's flattering reply, adding, 'It would be difficult to decide whether the speeches of his Lordship, or your Ladyship's songs were to be most admired by those who had the pleasure of hearing them.' His remarks might well prompt one to speculate that he could perhaps rival Sir William's talents in the delicate art of diplomacy!

As well as being in business as a printer, Heath was a prolific writer on local history and topography, and proudly presented the visitors with copies of his latest book, *A Description of Monmouthshire*. Shortly after their visit, he published his *Descriptive Account of the Kymin Pavilion and Naval Temple*, which included the following illuminating details of his meeting with Nelson. 'The feelings of that man are not to be envied, who could receive with coldness such a mark of attention, from a nobleman who might be deemed the pride

*The summer house in Col. Lindsay's garden where Nelson and his friends retired for after-dinner coffee. It still stands in the garden at the rear of 18 Monnow Street. Courtesy: Nelson Museum, Monmouth.*

*Before leaving Monmouth, Nelson and the Hamiltons walked through the town viewing objects of interest including the medieval gateway that spans the Monnow Bridge. From an original oil painting by John Arthur Evans.*

and glory of his country. On receiving the books, Lord Nelson thanked me in the most gracious manner, and taking off his hat, he laid it on the counter. Which drew from me the remark, that as monarchs had taken off their hats to his Lordship, it was impossible for him to remain uncovered in the presence of a country printer, and that he would permit me to replace it again on his head.' – which he did.

Since coming to Monmouth in 1791, Heath had busied himself writing his gossipy little guidebooks on the Wye Valley, and chronicling the interesting happenings in the district. He had a reporter's nose for a good story, and it was unlikely that there would ever be a story more interesting to the present and future generations in the town than the visit of the great Horatio Nelson. 'Vanity', he wrote, 'has no share whatever in detailing the conversations which passed at this interview – it has far better and more interesting motives.' He told Lord Nelson, that the company at dinner had been deeply gratified by his speeches, and asked permission to commit them to press. 'No, Mr. Heath, I am an old man and may not live long; it is my wish that posterity should know my sentiments – therefore do it.' Heath relates – 'I accordingly published them in a few days and for the first time, gave them a place in my collections.'

He goes on to relate:

Receiving so kind an answer, I was further induced to know from his Lordship, the truth or fallacy of an heroic action, said to have been performed by him off Cape St.Vincent, on the 14th February 1797, with the Spanish fleet, which had often appeared to me as an instance of the greatest valour, recorded among the brightest achievements of his memorable life. In consequence of which I then said, it would very much increase obligations, if he would permit me to ask him another question, to which his Lordship replied, that I might ask as many as I pleased. I mentioned that I had seen a print representing his Lordship in the above glorious action, after capturing the Santissima Trinidada, boarding another of the enemy's ships by following a marine along the bowsprit of his vessel, and jumping into the San Josef at the quarter gallery window. I enquired if the circumstance was founded on fact 'It is very true' was his Lordship's immediate reply. 'The man went in first, and I followed him.' I was also particular in enquiring if his Lordship ever knew who the gallant fellow was, and whether, like another Alexander, he lived to fight the battle o'er again? But he only repeated the answer, that all he knew was that the man was a private soldier belonging to the 69th Regiment of Foot, doing duty as a marine, and that in such moments, every person was too much engaged in his own duty to be acquainted with the fortunes of others. But when his Lordship left my house, and joined again in conversation, he observed to Mr. Hollings, on whose arm he rested – 'Since Mr. Heath has challenged my memory, I have a better recollection of the circumstance to which he alludes. Two men left the ship with me, but one of them fell into the sea; the other, as soon as he got near the end of the bowsprit, knocked in with the butt end of his musket, the quarter gallery windows of the enemy vessel, and jumped through them into the ship as I followed. The soldier, besides his musket, had some other dreadful instrument of death, and when he met the enemy, used it with such fury, that I soon after exclaimed to him mercy! mercy! stop! and immediately the Spaniards surrendered up their ship.'

The romantic Mr. Heath concluded: 'Hence it may be said, that by the daring spirit of a British private soldier, this vessel was almost instantly wrested from the power of the enemy, and its commander laid prostrate at the conqueror's feet.'

Heath frequently reported on local events for the *Hereford News & Journal* and the *Gloucester Journal,* in which the Monmouth visit was fully chronicled. Copies of the papers were sent to Nelson at Merton, for which he received the following letter of acknowledgement.

Merton                                                    September 14th 1802

Sir,
Lady Hamilton and myself beg leave to return you our thanks for

*Charles Heath, the Monmouth writer, printer and bookseller who met Nelson and chronicled the visit to the town. Courtesy: Monmouth Museum.*

*Monmouth's Agincourt Square in the  d-nineteenth century. Heath's shop was on the left of the picture, opposite the  ire Hall. Courtesy: Monmouth Museum.*

your kind attention to our wishes, in sending the newspapers and my speech; which although it flowed immediate from the heart, was but ill suited to meet the eye of the public, except those partial friends at Monmouth, to whom we, with Sir William, Dr. & Mrs. Nelson, beg to be remembered with the utmost esteem, and I beg you to believe that I feel myself

Your much obliged and obedient servant,

Nelson & Bronte

Soon after leaving Heath's shop, the visitors left the peaceful market town of Monmouth, which now stood prouder than ever on that 'little gut of a river called the Wye.' They had admired the beauty of its situation, been impressed by the challenging medieval gateway on the Monnow Bridge, and were reminded by the statue of King Henry V in Agincourt Square of the town's royal connection. Now the name of Nelson would be woven with his into the tapestry of this historic borough.

They returned to Ross-on-Wye by carriage and, thinking they might pass through the town unnoticed, entered it on a quiet by-road, but to no avail. News of Nelson's impending arrival had once again brought the crowds out in their hundreds. So, bowing to popular demand, the carriages were diverted into the main street where a triumphal arch of oak and laurel had been erected with an appropriate inscription in praise of the gallant admiral. Driving beneath the arch, the visitors made for the historic manor house of Rudhall, home of Mr. and Mrs. Thomas Westfaling who were friends of the Hamiltons from their Naples days. Mary Westfaling was mistress of Rudhall Manor, which she had inherited in 1792, and on her marriage to Thomas Brereton he assumed her name and adopted her family coat of arms. The travellers remained at Rudhall for three days, where Nelson was accommodated in the the Chapel Room above the ante-chapel.[63]

A dinner was given on the evening of their arrival, to which the Westfalings invited a number of friends. One rather surprising guest was the Danish Baron Anker, whom Nelson recognised as one of the signatories of the treaty following the Battle of Copenhagen. The two former adversaries expressed mutual astonishment at meeting in such unlikely circumstances, and spent some time in friendly conversation. The baron was an industrialist, making his way into South Wales, and was particularly interested in Crawshay's iron works at Merthyr Tydfil, which doubtless provided the two men with an interesting topic of conversation over an after-dinner glass of vintage port.

There were 'oohs' and 'ahs' as the night skies over Rudhall glowed with the colourful and noisy display of fireworks which preceded a grand ball that went on into the early hours of the following day. Though the energetic Emma may well have persuaded her lover to dance with her through the warm summer night, it is likely that the retiring Sir William had been abed many an hour by the time the guests dispersed in the dawn light. As they did so, several hogsheads of cider were liberally dispensed to the hundreds of spectators who had stayed on to witness this great gala occasion, the like of which had never been seen in Ross before, and was not likely to be seen there again.

Reports of the tour continued to filter back to the London press, and the *Morning Post* was, as always, ready to give the story a mildly humorous twist with an amusing reference to the nation's habit of naming just about everything after its bravest son. 'There is no man so busily employed in England as Lord Nelson. In one place we see him as a gooseberry, in another as a carnation – sometimes as a racehorse, and sometimes as a prize ram!'[64]

News of Nelson's presence in the county had reached the mayor of Hereford who, not wishing to be upstaged by the little town of Ross, promptly headed a delegation of civic leaders to wait on his lordship at Rudhall. They took with them an invitation for the admiral and his friends to favour their city with a visit, and accept its freedom.

The party arrived at Hereford on Monday 23 August, and

*Rudhall Manor where Nelson and the Hamiltons were the guests of Thomas and Mary Westfaling. The visitors were accommodated in the wing on the right of the picture. From an original drawing by Haydn Barrington.*

*The Wye Bridge at Hereford where Nelson was greeted by a great multitude of admirers. Courtesy: Hereford County Archives.*

were greeted at Wye Bridge by a great multitude of admirers and well wishers, all eager to snatch a glimpse of this great little man. The carriages were brought to a halt and the horses removed, as a band of brawny Hereford boys stepped forward to yoke themselves into the vehicles which were towed ceremoniously through the streets to Mr. Bennett's Hotel in Broad Street. By now, the cheering and shouting had reached a crescendo as the people swarmed around the carriages in a popular demonstration of the affection that Nelson had experienced throughout the tour. It was these tumultuous manifestations of his popularity, that prompted the *Morning Post* to comment – 'It is a singular fact that more eclat attends Lord Nelson in his provincial rambles, than attends the King.'

Inside the hotel they were received on behalf of the city by the Lord Chief Steward, Charles Howard, 11th Duke of Norfolk, and one wonders what the visitors made of this eccentric nobleman. Nicknamed 'The Jockey', he is said to have been immensely obese, obscene, plethoric and crafty-eyed. He wore shabby old clothes with a greasy black hat, and there was nothing in his appearance to suggest the regal state he maintained at Arundel and London. His Duchess was the former Miss Scudamore, a wealthy heiress of Holme Lacey, near Hereford who, perhaps not surprisingly, went mad and was put away shortly after their marriage.

Gross and gluttonous, he would devour enormous beef-steaks and drink great drafts of wine from a huge silver tankard. His aversion to soap and water was such that the servants had to take advantage of his drunken stupors to bath him. When he complained to Dudley North that he suffered from rheumatism and had in vain tried every cure known to man, North enquired cynically, 'Pray my lord, did you ever try a clean shirt?' Yet, in spite of his peculiar life-style, there was another side to the Duke's character; he was widely recognised as a cultured man of considerable knowledge and taste, and was a President of the Royal Society of Arts.[65]

The Duke ceremoniously conducted the visitors to the Town Hall, where Nelson's name was added to the roll of freemen of the city of Hereford. It was an occasion that provided yet another field day for the more sensational sections of the press, where it was incorrectly reported that 'The branch of an apple tree in full bearing, being presented to Lord Nelson at Hereford, his Lordship, with all the gallantry of Paris, presented the apple to Lady Hamilton, thereby acknowledging her Ladyship a perfect Venus.'[66] The freedom scroll was, in fact, presented in an applewood box by the town clerk, Mr. Lacon Lamb, who addressed the new freeman on behalf of the city:

My Lord, By the permission of our noble Lord Chief Steward, His Grace the Duke of Norfolk, I have the particular honour of addressing your Lordship on behalf of the Mayor, Alderman and Citizens, and to attempt to express, though very inadequate, the great honour we feel in your gracious visit to this City.

We look with wonder, as well at your own intrepid courage, as your cool conduct and humanity in the many signal victories you have gained for your country, in whose preservation you have had so eminent a share, both in delivering her from impending ruin, and exalting her to that pitch of glory and greatness in which she now shines amid the states of Europe.

In a particular manner we are impressed with admiration at your Lordship's humility on the day of battle, and in the very flush of victory in wholly divesting yourself of all the glory, so justly your due, and ascribing to Him, whose will determines the fate of battles and the fate of nations, all the honour of praise for the success of those great events! You have by your conduct my Lord, fully evinced your worthy descent, and that in your veins flows some of the blood of your great and pious ancestors, whose writings will be the study and consolation of all good Christians in this country to the end of time.

Your honour and fame, my Lord are so completely full, and even overflowing, that though all we may attempt to add to them is but as the dust upon the scale, or a drop in the ocean, yet we are emulous of casting in our poor mite, as well to yours

*Charles Howard, 11th Duke of Norfolk, the eccentric Lord Chief Steward of Herefordshire. Courtesy: Gloucester City Library.*

*Hereford Market Place and Town Hall where Nelson was presented with the City's Freedom contained in a box made from apple wood. Courtesy: Hereford City Library.*

as our own fame, by having your name enrolled among the Citizens of this ancient and loyal City, which will be a never failing honour to it. Accept then great Sir, this small suffrage of our gratitude, enclosed in a box of that tree, which is the pride of this County, and of whose noble juice many libations will not fail to be offered to the long health, prosperity and happiness of the great and glorious conqueror of the Nile.

Amid thunderous applause, Nelson stepped forward to receive the applewood box containing the freedom of the city from the town clerk, and after reading the inscription:

August XXIII M DCCCII
Lord Nelson Made An Honorary
Freeman of Hereford

pressed the box to his lips, and thanked the mayor and corporation for an honour that he would never forget. It was true that he had stood forward in the defence of his king and country in many engagements, yet the honour and renown for the brilliant victories which the fleets under him had obtained were, he said, not attributable to himself, but must be ascribed first to the Deity, and next, to the undaunted courage, skill and discipline of those officers and seamen, which it had been his good fortune to command, not one of whom, he was proud to say, had ever in the least swerved from his duty.

He went on to pay tribute to the loyalty and the patriotism of the people, saying 'Should this nation ever again experience a similar state to that from which it has been recently extricated, I have not the slightest doubt, from the results of my observations during this tour, that the native, the in-bred spirit of Britons, whilst it continues as firmly united as it is at present, is fully adequate successfully to repel any attack, either foreign or domestic, which our enemies may dare to make. You have but to say to your fleets and armies, "Go ye forth and fight your battles, whilst we, true to ourselves, protect and support our wives and little ones at home."'[67]

As might be expected, the speech was rapturously received by his audience, and just what they wanted to hear. Though it had not varied much from the many similar speeches made on the tour, it was delivered with sincere conviction, and came straight from the heart.

The civic formalities over, Nelson returned with his friends to the hotel, where they spent some time in the Great Room to afford him a further opportunity of meeting the people. One person who had not been present at the freedom ceremony was the bishop of Hereford, who sent a message regretting that due to infirmity, he was unable to attend. Nelson made a kindly reply, saying that as the son of a clergyman he sincerely regretted the cause of the bishop's absence, and considered it a duty to wait on the prelate at the palace, which he did before leaving for Ludlow.

They continued on the northward road to Leominster, which took them on a pleasant route through Herefordshire's fertile cider country, abundant in tree-laden apple orchards. Crossing the River Teme by the old stone bridge, they entered the little Shropshire market town of Ludlow, where the now familiar jubilant demonstrations of adulation awaited them. Once again, men emerged from the crowds to take over from the horses, drawing the carriages through the streets at a processional pace to the Crown Inn. One eye-witness who many years later penned her recollections of the event was Mrs. Stackhouse Acton, a niece of Richard Payne Knight, the town's Whig member of parliament with whom the visitors were to spend some lazy days away from the noise of the admiring hordes. 'I have a recollection of being held up in my nurse's arms, to see Lord Nelson who was standing at an open window at the Crown Inn at Ludlow with another gentleman and a lady, who I suppose were Sir William and Lady Hamilton. They were on the way to visit my uncle at Downton Castle.'[68]

The scholarly Payne Knight was a renowned intellectual, well-versed in Latin and Greek, and a friend of the poet Goethe. He had travelled extensively in Europe, and first

*A Hereford street scene in the early nineteenth century. Courtesy: Hereford County Archives.*

*Downton Castle, home of Richard Payne Knight. Courtesy: Hereford City Library.*

met Sir William Hamilton in Italy. Both men shared a deep interest in classical antiquity and, like Nelson, he was the son of a country parson. From his grandfather, who had amassed a great fortune as an ironmaster at Coalbrookdale, he inherited the large estate at Downton a few miles to the south-west of Ludlow. There, in 1776, he had built a mock medieval castle where he lived in a state of splendid affluence. Payne Knight was an acknowledged expert in the art of landscaping and had designed the gardens and parklands at Downton. He must have been very sure of his knowledge and skill as a landscape artist, for on a visit to Bowood House in Wiltshire with his friend Sir Uvedale Price, he provoked the wrath of its owner Lord Lansdown with his critical observations of the landscaping. Perhaps Lord Lansdown's indignation was understandable, since the work had been executed, no doubt at great expense, by the man generally regarded as being England's greatest landscape artist, Capability Brown.[69]

It seems that Lady Hamilton had let it be known that the party would be travelling in the vicinity of Ludlow during the tour, for on arriving at Monmouth on the previous Thursday, a letter awaited her, dated Sunday 15 August 1802, from Richard Payne Knight, inviting the party to stay at Downton.

I do assure you, my dear Lady Hamilton, that nothing will give me more real concern than that you and my friend Sir William should come into this country and not take up your abode at Downton; and, though I have not the honour of being personally acquainted with Lord Nelson, I beg to assure him that I shall be equally flattered and gratified in his company; indeed, I should think myself a very unnatural and ungrateful Englishman, if I felt otherwise.

As, however, your laconic epistle does not tell me when you go to Lord Cawdor's, or when you leave it, or when you are to be at Monmouth or Ludlow, I cannot guess the time when I may hope to see you. I will therefore give you a statement of my own engagements, trusting to you to arrange matters so as to come between them. During the whole of the ensuing week my house will be filled with W. Spencer, Lord Cowper, and a large party, and towards the end of the month I expect the whole Abercorn family, who will fill it again for about a fortnight; but from about ye 22nd to 28th I shall probably be alone, or nearly so, and at all events, happy to see you.

As you do not tell me where Mr. Morris's or Clasemont is, I shall enclose this to Lord Nelson at Monmouth, taking it for granted that it cannot fail to find so distinguished a person, wherever he may happen to be. Your letter having however, been a week in coming here, I doubt whether it will come to you in time, I shall therefore send another to Mr. Buckley's (Bulkeley) at Ludlow to waylay you there.[70]

The letter from Payne Knight was not the only one Emma received during the prolonged excursion. The strain of the long journey made in uncomfortable carriages on roads that were often little more that dirt tracks was taking its toll of the elderly Sir William. So too was the hectic round of social engagements, the late nights and Nelson's habit of rising early and taking to the road before breakfast. With his energetic young wife constantly lavishing attention on her heroic lover, Sir William's tolerance was, like his body, being tested to the point of exhaustion. It was enough to tax the energies of a man half his age and would have tested the tolerance of a saint. With barely a moment of privacy, it was almost impossible to confront Emma in person, so he resorted to communicating with her in writing. One of these notes, exchanged in August 1802, probably about the time they were at Swansea, has survived, and it is clear that having accomplished the purpose of his visit to Milford, he would have been content to take the shortest route back to Merton:

I neither love bustle or great company, but I like some employment and diversion. I have but a very short time to live, and every moment is precious to me. I am in no hurry, and am exceedingly glad to give every satisfaction to our best friend,

*Richard Payne Knight of Downton Castle. Courtesy: Whitworth Art Gallery, Manchester.*

*Broad Street, Ludlow in the early nineteenth century. Courtesy: Mr Peter Egan.*

our dear Lord Nelson. The question, then, is what we can do that all may be perfectly satisfied. Sea bathing is useful to your health; I see it is, and wish you to continue it a little longer; but I must confess that I regret whilst the season is favourable, that I cannot enjoy my favourite amusement of quiet fishing. I care not a pin for the great world, and am attached to no one so much as to you.

The busy Emma gave the note short shrift, returning it with a scribbled message on the back. 'I go when you tell me the coach is ready', to which Sir William despairingly retorted: 'This is not a fair answer to a fair confession of mine.'[71]

In spite of the stresses and strains now being experienced by some members of the party in private, there seems to have been no public manifestation of the discontent other than Emma's apparent neglect of her husband. Perhaps a few quiet days in the stimulating company of Payne Knight, with an opportunity to tempt the trout on the River Teme, might help to relieve some of Sir William's boredom, but for Emma and Nelson there was no let-up. They took a carriage to Pencombe, near Bromyard to visit the vicar, the Rev. Herbert Glass, who was Nelson's godfather, and to call on his old seafaring friend, Richard Bulkeley, with whom he had served on HMS *Hinchingbrooke* during the San Juan River Expedition of 1780. It was an ill-fated adventure in which many died, and of the *Hinchingbrooke*'s two hundred men, only ten survived. In 1797, Bulkeley called on Nelson at his Bond Street lodgings, taking his two sons with him. There was much talk of naval matters, and Nelson thrilled the boys when he showed them his sword. The encounter made such a strong impression on Bulkeley's youngest son, Dick, then aged nine, that some three years later his parents intercepted a letter he had written to Nelson, offering to serve in the navy. Before despatching the letter, the boy's father added a footnote: 'As you have bit him, you must be his physician.'[72]

69

Young Dick Bulkeley's enthusiasm for the navy remained undiminished and as soon as he was old enough, he fulfilled his long-cherished ambition by enlisting. Like the boy Roteley of Swansea, Bulkeley junior served on HMS *Victory* at Trafalgar, where he witnessed the historic drama of Nelson's heroic death. As the Admiral lay mortally wounded, he begged for Captain Hardy to be brought to him. 'Will no one bring Hardy to me?' he gasped. 'He must be killed.' As the greatest sea battle in British naval history raged about them, a fresh faced youth, who had himself been wounded, came below decks carrying an urgent message to his dying commander. The young lieutenant was to tell the stricken Nelson that Captain Hardy's presence was required at his post on deck, but that he would seize the first available opportunity to come down to his Lordship. 'Who brought me that message?' he enquired of the purser. 'It is Mr. Bulkeley my Lord.' As his life ebbed away, Nelson recalled the name; perhaps he even recalled that happy day spent with his beloved Emma three summers before, deep in the tranquil peace of Pencombe, as he murmered – 'Remember me to your father.'[73] It was an awesome moment that the young naval lieutenant from Herefordshire would never forget.

On Saturday 25 August, the Salopian market town of Ludlow added Nelson's name to its roll of freemen, and on the following day the celebrated visitors embarked on a further stage of their homeward trek. At Tenbury Wells on the way to Worcester, the local newspaper reported that on their arrival in the town the people drew the coaches over the bridge, up into the town, and back again.[74] Shortly after leaving Tenbury, some problems were encountered with one of the carriages, requiring them to return to the little Temeside town for repairs. That done, they continued on their carefree way, down dusty lanes flanked by fertile fields of hop bines that would soon yield to the busy fingers of the families that each year came into the countryside from nearby towns to reap the harvest.

They journeyed through the Worcestershire countryside, now bathed in the warm August sunshine, and were waved at, cheered at and stared at all along the way, as the bells of every village church rang out in joyful celebration. It was an unbelievable, once in a lifetime opportunity for these humble countryfolk of Britain to share for a fleeting moment in the glorious triumph of the man who had saved their country.

# SIX

WORCESTER – DROITWICH – BROMSGROVE –
BIRMINGHAM – WARWICK – COVENTRY –
ALTHORP – DAVENTRY – TOWCESTER –
DUNSTABLE – ST. ALBANS – WATFORD –
BRENTFORD – MERTON PLACE

The menacing noise of cannon fired in salute signalled the Admiral's arrival in Worcester, as the city's churches joined with cathedral bells to proclaim Nelson's presence. Throughout the day excitement had been mounting in anticipation of his arrival so that by the time he entered the city the pent-up enthusiasm erupted into an immense demonstration of patriotic fervour. Men, women and children hung from upstairs windows and every available vantage point along the route to get a good view of the carriage bearing the hero, now wearing a glittering assortment of medals and decorations, being drawn through a surging sea of flag-waving citizens. Slowly they progressed along Broad Street and the Cross to Foregate Street where the vehicles were brought to a halt outside the 'Hop Pole', then one of the city's principal inns on this busy coaching route. Crowds collected daily at the 'Hop Pole' to witness the rapid changes of horses, with particular interest focusing on the two deadly rivals that covered the Liverpool to Bristol route, *Hibernia* and *Hirondelle*. They were reckoned to be two of the fastest coaches ever to run, and raced each other all the way.[75] But today there were thousands gathered outside the inn, where they remained late into the night, calling for the great Lord Nelson to make an appearance, which he frequently did, gracefully bowing to acknowledge their plaudits and to gratify their insatiable demands.

*A view of Worcester, looking south from the banks of the River Severn, with the porcelain factory on the left. Courtesy: Clive and Malcolm Haynes.*

*The Hop Pole Inn on Foregate Street, where Nelson stayed on his visit to Worcester. Courtesy: Mr H.W. Gwilliam.*

*There was some surprise that Nelson was taken to Mr Chamberlain's china factory at Diglis, rather than the better known Worcester Porcelain Factory. Courtesy: Dyson Perrins Museum Trust.*

*A plate from the breakfast service ordered at Chamberlains, decorated with Nelson's coat of arms, and bearing the motto 'Tria Juncta In Uno'. Courtesy: Dyson Perrins Trust.*

On Monday morning, the visitors were conducted from the Inn by the landlord, Mr. Weaver, who invited them to walk with him in a procession behind a band to Mr. Chamberlain's China Factory at Diglis. Some surprise was expressed that such important visitors had not been taken to the City's principal and better-known factory, but as Mr. Weaver had arranged the excursion, and Mr. Chamberlain was his friend, his preference prevailed. Nelson entered the factory through an arch of laurel decorated with an elegant blue flag bearing an inscription in his honour.[76]

There was tremendous excitement as the workers proudly demonstrated their skills and the various processes involved in producing some of the world's finest china. One young man from the Staffordshire Potteries who had recently joined Chamberlain's as a decorative artist was James Plant who, many years later, recalled how a very battered-looking gentleman entered the paint shop. 'He had lost an arm and an eye, and leaning on his left and only arm, was the beautiful Lady Hamilton, who was evidently pleased at the interest excited by her companion. A number of other people followed behind them, including a very infirm old gentleman; this was Sir William Hamilton'. After touring the factory for about an hour, talking to the employees and showing an absorbing interest in their work they went to the shop in High Street to inspect the large selection of porcelain. Nelson was impressed with its quality and remarked that although he possessed the finest porcelain that the courts of Dresden and Naples could afford, he had seen nothing to compare with what he had seen at Chamberlain's. Before leaving, Sir William and Lady Hamilton made liberal purchases of porcelain, and Nelson gave a large order, to be decorated with his coat of arms, which was confirmed by the following entry in Chamberlain's order book:

The Right Hon Lord Nelson, Duke of Bronte,
No.23, Piccadilly, opposite the Green Park

1802 August 27th

12  Large breakfast cups and saucers
12  Small ditto
12  Coffees and saucers
2  Slop basins
4  Bread plates
2  Water plates and covers
2  Sugar boxes
2  Teapots and stands
2  Milk jugs
12  Cake plates
5  Small dishes
6  Egg cups
6  Drainers
2  Butter tubs
2  Beehives
6  Chocolates, 2 handles, covers and stands
1  Complete dinner service
1  Complete dessert service with ice pails
1  Elegant vase, richly decorated with a miniature of His
    Lordship supported by a figure of fame
1  Ditto with a likeness of Lady Hamilton
1  Cup and saucer ditto

There is more than a suggestion of Emma's influence and
extravagance in the order, and perhaps also a hint of
Nelson's vanity. In the event, only the breakfast service was
completed before Nelson's death at Trafalgar three years
later, and although most of it ultimately found its way into
the hands of collectors, five pieces are known to have
survived, and are now in the Worcester Porcelain Museum.

Lunch was taken with the mayor and corporation of
Worcester at the Town Hall, where the Earl of Coventry
presented Lord Nelson with a richly ornamented china vase
containing the city's freedom scroll. In a short speech,

74

*The Thrower and the Kiln Placing House. There was tremendous excitement as the workers proudly demonstrated their skills.*
*Courtesy: Dyson Perrins Trust.*

*The Painting Room and Dipping Room. James Plant recalled how a very battered-looking gentleman entered the Paint Shop: 'He had lost an arm and an eye and leaning on his left and only arm was the beautiful Lady Hamilton.'*

Nelson declined to take the credit for his great naval victories, saying that the merit should be ascribed to the brave men who served under him, and it was to them that the country was indebted; he had only the good fortune to command the heroes. He pledged that his remaining years would be devoted to his king, and while he had a limb left, that limb would be cheerfully sacrificed.[77]

There was still the occasional embarrassing incident involving Emma. It is not possible to be entirely certain what occurred at Worcester but it seems that Nelson was furious with 'those damned glover women', who were said to have been very aloof with her Ladyship. Sir William's annoyance is not recorded, but maybe by now he was past caring, and perhaps it was to make amends that her ladyship was presented with a bound volume of *The Life of Don Quixote*. By now, the carriages must have been straining under the weight of the gifts, souvenirs and a variety of receptacles containing freedom scrolls, collected from various towns and boroughs along the way. Mr. Michael, a local carpet maker added to the gifts with a pair of bedside carpets, and in addition to the porcelain, a large quantity of cider and perry was taken on board at Worcester, costing an indulgent £12. 16s. 0d.[78]

Leaving on what is now the A38 road, they were cheered through Droitwich and Bromsgrove on their way to Styles Hotel in Birmingham, where they arrived at 5.30pm. News of Nelson's presence quickly spread through the city, as the crowds again began to mass outside the hotel, chanting 'We want Nelson'. The *Coventry Mercury* reported that in response to the demands of the people, 'His Lordship affably gratified by repeatedly appearing at the windows when he was often saluted with the most enthusiastic shouts of admiration and applause; and while every anxious eye beamed with pleasure, and every heart overflowed with gratitude, the bells rang a merry peal, to welcome the Hero of the Nile to the Toy Shop of Europe.'[79]

In the evening, the whole party left the hotel to go to the

theatre for a performance of *The Merry Wives Of Windsor*, but instead of two horse-drawn carriages awaiting them, a body of hardy Birmingham men was once again ready to supply the 'horse power', and the carriages were dragged through the streets in a somewhat disorderly but good-natured procession. As Nelson entered the building, the capacity audience came to its feet to join the band in a lusty rendering of *Rule Britannia*.[80]

One youngster who witnessed it all was the theatre manager's son, W.C. Macready, who later became a famous actor, and for posterity, he wrote it all down in his diary.

But one evening (in giving me a sight of the man with whose fame all Europe rang, and who will ever rank first among our country's naval heros) stands out in my memory as marked with golden letters. During the short peace of Amiens, Nelson made a tour through several of our provincial towns – a recreation apparently innocent enough, but which was harshly reflected on in the House of Lords. Birmingham was one of those he visited, and I believe my memory does not err in stating that the people drew his carriage, or attempted to draw it from the suburbs to his hotel. The news of his arrival spread like wildfire, and when his intention of going to the theatre got wind, all who heard of it, as might have been expected, flocked there to behold and do him honour.'

The play was Shakespeare's 'Merry Wives of Windsor' for the benefit of a player of the name of Blisset, who had some repute in the part of Falstaff. At my father's request Lord Nelson consented to bespeak for the next night the play of 'King Henry IVth', wishing to see Blisset again in Falstaff. The box office was literally besieged early the next morning and every place soon taken. At the hour of commencement, my father was waiting with candles to conduct the far famed hero through the lobby, which went round the whole semi circle of the lower tier to his box. The shouts outside announced the approach of the carriage; the throng was great, but being close to my father's side, I had not only a perfect view of the Hero's pale and interesting face, but

*A panoramic view of Birmingham in the early nineteenth century. Reproduced by permission: Reference Library Local Studies Department, Birmingham City Library.*

*The celebrated actor W.C. Macready as Werner. As a boy, Macready was present when Nelson and the Hamiltons attended his father's Birmingham Theatre. Glyn Vivien Art Gallery, Swansea.*

listened with such eager attention to every word he uttered, that I had all he said by heart, and for months afterwards was wont to be called on to repeat 'what Lord Nelson said to your father.'

Nothing of course passed unnoticed by my boyish enthusiasm: the right arm empty sleeve attached to his breast, the Orders upon it, a sight to me so novel and remarkable; but the melancholy expression of his countenance, and extremely mild and gentle tones of his voice impressed me most sensibly. They were indeed for a life's remembrance. When with Lady Hamilton and Dr. Nelson, he entered his box the uproar of the house was deafening and seemed as if it would know no end. The play was at length suffered to proceed, after which was a sort of divertisment in honour of the illustrious visitor, from one song of which I can even now recollect one couplet! Oh sacred nine forgive me while I quote it!

'We'll shake hands and be friends; if they won't why, what then? We'll send our brave Nelson to thrash 'em again.'

The crowded house was frantic in its applause at this sublime effusion. Lady Hamilton laughing loud and without stint clapped with uplifted hands and all her heart, and kicked with her heels against the foot-board of the seat, while Nelson placidly and with his mournful look (perhaps in pity for the poet) bowed repeatedly to the oft repeated cheers. Next day my father called at the hotel to thank his Lordship, when Nelson presented him with what he intended to be the cost of his box wrapped in paper, regretting that his ability to testify his respect for my father was so much below his will. My father never told me the amount, but purchased with it a piece of plate that he retained to his death in memory of the donor.

I should not omit to mention that in the hall of the hotel were several sailors of Nelson's ship waiting to see him, to each of whom the great Admiral spoke in the most affable manner, inquiringly and kindly, as he passed through to his carriage, and left them, I believe, some tokens of his remembrance.[81]

The *Coventry Mercury* reported that before going to the theatre in the evening, '. . . an elegant dinner consisting of every delicacy the season could afford, was provided by the

High and Low Bailiffs for his Lordship and his party, who were met by a number of respectable gentlemen among whom were Heneage Legge, Esq., the High Sheriff, Dugdale Stratford Dugdale Esq., (one of the Members for this County), Capt. Digby (who had the honour of being selected by Lord Nelson for his conveyance to Great Britain after his wonderful achievements), Colonel Mahan of the 7th Dragoon Guards, Colonel Carver, and the Magistrates. Lady Hamilton very condescendingly gratified the company with two most appropriate charming songs, and a gentleman of the party sang several delightful airs.'[82] Nelson was again mobbed as he left the theatre, and although it was past midnight, there were still thousands waiting to see him. By the light of hundreds of torches his carriage was drawn slowly through New Street, into High Street and along Bull Street to Styles Hotel, where the crowds stayed on into the early hours.

They were still there in their thousands on Tuesday morning when the whole visiting party, accompanied by the bailiffs and magistrates, left the hotel in the style of royalty to inspect some of the many manufacturing workshops for which nineteenth-century Birmingham was so renowned. First they went to Mr. Clay's Japan factory in Newhall Street, then on to Smith's to see how buttons were made. With swarms of people in their wake and the bells still ringing, they walked down Edmund Street to view the workshops of the sword-makers, Wolley and Deakins, before moving on to Livery Street and the buckle and ring workshop of Simcox and Timmins. The walkabout finished in St. Paul's Square where, through the crowds, they made for the premises of Timmins and Jordan, who described themselves as Patent Sash Makers.   There was no shortage of volunteers to tow the carriage to Mr. Eginton's stained glass factory at Handsworth, where they were welcomed by pretty young ladies who scattered their way with flower petals. They walked through the works, wondering at the craftsmanship and admiring the colourful windows made

*Right: The Birmingham industrialist, Matthew Boulton. Too ill to show Nelson over his Soho factory, he received the Admiral at his bedside. Below: Matthew Boulton's Soho Works. Reproduced by permission: Reference Library Local Studies Department, Birmingham City Library.*

*Warwick Castle, home of Charles Greville's parents, the Earl of Warwick, and his Countess Elizabeth, sister of Sir William Hamilton. Courtesy: Warwick County Reference Library.*

*An early nineteenth-century view of Coventry. Courtesy: Warwick County Reference Library.*

for the Duke of Norfolk's Arundel Castle, and the Fonthill home of Sir William's millionaire friend William Beckford. Finally, they called at Matthew Boulton's brass foundry in Soho, where commemorative medals were struck in honour of the visit. The infirm Mr. Boulton was unable to conduct them around the foundry himself, but was flattered to receive a bedside visit from the celebrated callers.

The visit to Birmingham ended on Wednesday 31 August, but not before they had watched pins being made, tramped through a toy warehouse, called at the workshops of Mr. Radenhurst who made whips, and finally, inspected the Blue Coat School where, it is said, the appearance of the children gave them much pleasure.[83] After two very full days in Birmingham, they left at one o'clock, bound for the county town of Warwick, where the whole populace turned out with the mayor and corporation to greet them. There seems to have been no sign of the presence in the welcoming party of the town's member of parliament, who was none other than the Hon. Charles Greville, second son of the Earl of Warwick, and his Countess Elizabeth, sister of Sir William Hamilton. Not for the first time on the tour, the party arrived without prior notice, and as both Lord and Lady Warwick were away from the castle, the travellers had to make do with the modest accomodation offered by the Warwick Arms Inn.

The churchwarden of St. Mary's noted in his accounts that by order of the mayor, the ringers were given a guinea 'for ringing for Lord Nelson at Warwick.' A little further on, he records the Trafalgar celebrations: 'Nov. 7th 1805 – gave the ringers for Nelson's victory, £1. 1s. 0d.', but by 23 November 1805, news of Nelson's death had reached the town, and a sadder entry on 23 November tells of Nelson's death: 'Gave the ringers for tolling and buffing the bells one hour for Lord Nelson's burial – 10 shillings.' During their stay at Warwick, the tourists did call at the castle and, much to the delight of the townsfolk, occupied the rest of their time in sightseeing. The tour was now drawing to an end and on Saturday, after an overnight stop at Coventry's King's Head Inn, they proceeded to Althorp Park near Northampton to call on George, 2nd Earl Spencer, ancestor of the present Princess of Wales.

Lord Spencer was formerly First Lord of The Admiralty, and both Nelson and Sir William had cause to be grateful to him. He had been among the first to recognise the genius of the young naval officer, and was instrumental in securing his first important appointment. He had also recognised the potential of Milford Haven and encouraged its development by placing orders there for Royal Navy ships, and doubtless both Sir William and Lord Nelson would have much to tell his lordship.

The road home lay straight down Watling Street through Towcester, Dunstable and St. Albans, taking a tired and happy party back to Merton Place, where they arrived on Sunday 5 September 1802. Thus ended a long and exhausting tour through England and Wales, a tour that had been nothing short of a triumph for the nation's hero. It had served to demonstrate to Nelson the love and affection with which he was regarded throughout the length and breadth of the land, perhaps most importantly, by the ordinary folk for whose freedom he had fought so gallantly. On 11 September, he wrote to his friend Davison, confiding: 'Our tour has been very fine and interesting, and the way in which I have been everywhere received most flattering to my feelings, and although some of the higher powers may wish to keep me down, yet the reward of the general approbation and gratitude for my Services is an ample reward for all I have done, but it makes a comparison fly up to my mind, not much to the credit of some in the higher offices of state.'[84]

*George, 2nd Earl Spencer, a First Lord of the Admiralty who was responsible for Nelson's first important appointment. Courtesy: Northampton County Reference Library.*

*Althorp, the Northamptonshire home of the Earl Spencer and one of the last ports of call on the way back to Merton. Courtesy: Northampton County Reference Library.*

*The grand staircase at Althorp. Courtesy: Northampton County Reference Library.*

# SEVEN

# The End of The 'Tria Juncta in Uno'

Within a year, Sir William was to make his last long journey back to Pembrokeshire, but this time alone. Since returning from Wales he had divided his time between Merton and his London home and had even managed to do a little fishing on the Thames. The winter months were spent attending meetings of various societies, and he even took the chair for a sick colleague at a meeting of the Royal Society. But he was still plagued by money worries, and complained to Greville of Emma's 'shameful extravagance', which was aggravated by the continuing procession of house guests and her growing appetite for drink. This, and a third inhospitable English winter, which he found increasingly hard to bear after thirty-seven years of Italian sun, was about to take its final toll of the old ambassador. In March 1803, he collapsed at Merton, and and was taken back to his home at 23 Piccadilly. His condition rapidly deteriorated, and on the morning of April 6 he passed peacefully away, cradled in Emma's arms, as Nelson held his hand. The 'Tria Juncta in Uno' was at an end.

The funeral arrangements were carried out according to his will. 'First, to fulfil the promise I made to my excellent wife Katherine, Lady Hamilton (deceased) I desire my body to be deposited near hers in the family vault of the Barlows in Slebech Church in the County of Pembroke.' Here, the brief entry in the Parish Register simply recorded: 'Sir William Hamilton, 73 years, natural decay.' The will made adequate provision for his widow, and to his dear friend

81

Lord Nelson, he left a picture of Emma. The house in Piccadilly was, with the rest of Sir William's estate, inherited by the heartless Greville who gave his former mistress just one month to quit, and she quickly moved to some modest rented accomodation in nearby Clarges Street.

The brief uneasy peace between England and France was showing every sign of coming to an end, as the clouds of war once more began to gather. Having assured the Prime Minister – 'Whenever it is necessary, I am your Admiral,' the dutiful Nelson was soon on board HMS *Amphion*, heading for the Mediterranean to take command of his new flagship, *Victory*. It was more than two years before he returned to Merton for the last time, at six o'clock on the morning of 20 August 1805, having travelled overnight from Portsmouth. Conscious of Nelson's devotion to his family, Emma had gathered together the William Nelsons, the Boltons and the Matchams, and perhaps most important of all, their daughter Horatia, to complete the family homecoming.

The next twenty-five days were to be his last with Emma, and his last in England. Between visits to the Admiralty and meetings with various important officers of state in London, he contrived to spend as much time as possible with family and friends at Merton. After much discussion with the Prime Minister and senior colleagues at the Admiralty, he was given command of the Mediterranean Fleet, to the delight of his old friend Lord Minto who wrote to his wife:

> I met Nelson today in a mob in Piccadilly, and got hold of his arm, so that I was mobbed too. It is really quite affecting to see the wonder and admiration, and love and respect , of the whole world; and the genuine expression of all these sentiments at once, from gentle and simple, the moment he is seen. It is beyond anything represented in a play or a poem of fame.[85]

Minto dined at Merton on 12 September; his admiration for the admiral still as strong as his dislike of Lady

Hamilton. On the following day, the drama of Nelson's last hours with his loved ones in the only home he had ever owned was played out. He took his usual morning stroll through the grounds, pausing for a friendly word with the old gardener, Thomas Cribb. In the evening, Nelson sat down to an unusually quiet meal with Emma, his sister Kitty, and her husband George Matcham; there was none of the gaiety and laughter that characterised Emma's usual entertainment of her house guests. After dinner, he crept silently upstairs to the bedroom of the the sleeping child Horatia, to whisper a prayer and leave a farewell kiss. He had tried to comfort 'Brave Emma! Good Emma!' by telling her that 'If there were more Emmas, there would be more Nelsons,' but she found this of little consolation. At half-past-ten, he got into the waiting carriage and disappeared into the night on the long journey to join *Victory* at Portsmouth; he never saw Merton or his loved ones again, but left them a prayer in his private diary:

Friday night, at half-past-ten, drove from dear, dear Merton, where I left all which I hold dear in the world, to go to serve my King and Country. May the great God whom I adore, enable me to fulfil the expectations of my Country; and if it is His good pleasure that I should return, my thanks will never cease being offered up to the throne of His mercy. If is is His good Providence to cut short my days upon earth, I bow with the greatest submission, relying that He will protect those so dear to me, that I may leave behind. His will be done. Amen. Amen. Amen.[86]

News of Nelson's death was brought to Lady Hamilton at Merton on 6 November 1805 by a young naval officer who was near to tears, and quite unprepared for the hysterical reaction as she screamed uncontrollably before collapsing in a state of shock. Stunned by its loss, the nation mourned its greatest son, who had made the victory of Trafalgar more glorious by his own heroic death. Nelson's mortal remains were brought back to England and buried with all the honour that his country could bestow upon a hero. The coffin, made from the mainmast of the French ship L'Orient, and given to him by Captain Hallowel as a trophy, was used to contain his body, which was laid to rest beneath the great dome of St. Paul's Cathedral in a marble sarcophagus once intended for Cardinal Wolsey. In a codicil to his will, he had bequeathed Lady Hamilton as a legacy to his king and country – asking that they would give her an ample provision to maintain her rank in life. But it was not to be, for it was a legacy that no-one wanted. Emma Hamilton was now alone in the world, just how alone the coming months and years would cruelly tell.

Merton was sold, as were many of Nelson's relics, to pay off Emma's mounting debts. Many of the people who had once posed as her friends, and enjoyed the over-generous hospitality at Merton, now deserted her, and none more than the Rev. William Nelson from whom little of the milk of human kindness flowed. In recognition of his brother's service to the nation he was created Earl Nelson of Trafalgar, with an allowance of £5000 a year and a gift of £90,000 to purchase a house appropriate to his new rank. Even Nelson's sister Kitty received a pension of £2000 a year and £15,000 in cash, as did his estranged wife, but for the unfortunate Emma there was nothing. Homeless, she moved with Horatia from one rented lodging to another to avoid the pursuing creditors. Her careless life style and her addiction to drinking and gambling finally brought her before the King's Bench, and in 1813 she was committed to prison for debt. Ironically, she sought refuge in the bosom of the old enemy, France, when in 1814 she fled with her daughter to Calais. Here, from a primitive farmhouse she wrote to those in England who might feel inclined to relieve her penury. 'If there is humanity still left in British Hearts they will not suffer us to die of famine in a foreign country, for God's sake then send us some relief.' But it was to no avail. In rapidly failing health, she moved with Horatia into a squalid room at 27 Rue Française, where, broken-hearted, she died on 15 January 1815.

*The Death of Nelson on HMS Victory, 21st October 1805. An engraving from the painting by A.W. Devis. Courtesy: Nelson Museum, Monmouth.*

'If there is humanity still left in British Hearts they will not suffer us to die in a foreign country – for God's sake then send us some relief.' Emma Hamilton at Prayer, by George Romney. Courtesy: Eric Freeman.

Unlike Nelson's revered tomb, her obscure grave did not become a place of pilgrimage, but during the first World War a number of British army officers serving in France remembered this forgotten patriot, and raised sufficient money to place a memorial plaque on the house in Calais where she died, which read:

Emma, Lady Hamilton, the friend of Admiral Lord Nelson
died in this house, January 15th 1815
This tablet was erected by British Officers
Serving in Calais during the Great War
In memory of Lord Nelson's last Request
1918

Emily Lyon was, by any standards, a very remarkable woman. Often ill-used by the unscrupulous men in her life, she rose against the odds from the most humble obscurity to what even her detractors might consider to be an enviable position in society. There is no denying that she had faults, and the only person who seemed blind to her defects was Nelson – but as he said to Captain Foley, 'I have only one eye, and I have a right to be blind sometimes!' Sir William will be remembered as the husband of Emma Hamilton, while Emma and the heroic and indomitable Nelson, will be remembered for one of the greatest romances of all time.

# APENDIX A

*First draft of Lord Nelson's report on the Forest of Dean*

The Forest of Dean contains abt 23,000 Acres of the finest Land in the Kingdom which I am informed if in a high state of cultivation of Oak would produce abt 9200 loads of Timber fit for building Ships of the Line every year, that is the Forest would grow in full Vigor 920,000 Oak Trees

The State of the Forest at this moment is deplorable for if my information is true there is not 3500 Loads of Timber in the whole forest fit for building and none coming forward, It is useless I admit to state the causes of such want of Timber when so much could be produced except that by knowing the faults we may be better enabled to amend ourselves –,

first – the generality of trees for these last fifty years have been allowed to stand too long they are passed by instead of removed and thus occupy a space which ought to have been replanted with young trees,

secondly – that where good timber is felled nothing is planted and nothing can grow self sown for the Deer (of which now only a few remain) bark all the young trees, Vast Droves of Hogs are allowed to go into the Woods in the Autumn and if any fortunate acorn escapes their search and takes root, the flocks of sheep are allowed to go into the forest and they bite off the tender shoot, these are sufficient reasons why Timber does not grow in the Forest of Dean

Of the Waste of Timber in former times I can say nothing but of late years it has been I am told shameful, Trees are cut down in swampy places as the carriage is done by contract are left to rot and are cut by people in the neighbourhood, another abuse is the Contractors as they can carry more measurement are allowed to cut the trees to their advantage of carriage by which means the invaluable Crocked timber is lost for the service of the Navy

There is also another cause of the failure of timber, a sett of people called the forest free miners who consider themselves as having a right to dig for coal in any part they please these people in many places enclose pieces of ground which is daily encreasg by the inattention to call it by no worse name of the Surveyors Verdurers etc who have charge of the Forest

Of late years some apparently Vigorous measures were taken for preserving and encouraging the growth of Timber in the Kings Forests and part of the Forest of Dean has been enclosed but it is so very ill attended to that it is little if anything better than the other part

There is another abuse which I omitted to mention Trees which die of themselves are considered of no value, a Gentleman told me that in shooting on foot for on Horseback it cannot be seen, hid by the Fern which grows a great height the Trees of 50 years growth fit for building finering etc is cut just above ground entirely thro' the Bark in two years the tree dies and it becomes either a perquisite or is allowed to be taken away by favor'd people

These shameful abuses are probably known to those high in power but I have gathered the information of them from people of all discriptions and perfectly disinterested in telling me or knowing that I had any view in a trancient enquiry, But knowing the abuses it is for the serious consideration of every lover of this Country how they can either be done away or at least lessened perhaps a very difficult or impossible task,

If the Forest of Dean is to be preserved as a useful Forest for the Country strong measures must be pursued, 1st the Guardian of the support of Our Navy must be an Intelligent Honest Man who will give up his time to His Employment therefore he must live in the forest have a House a small farm and an adequate Salary,

I omitted to mention that the expence of Surveyor of Woods as far as relates to this Forest to be done away Verderer as at present also, The Guardian to have proper Verderers under him who understand the planting thining and management of Timber trees, There places should be so comfortable that the fear of being turn'd out should be a great Object of terror and of course an inducement for them to exert themselves in their different stations

The first thing necessary in the Forest of Dean is to plant some acres of acorns and I saw plenty of clear fields with Cattle grazing in my Voyage down the Wye, in two years these will be fit for transplanting

NB I am aware that Objections have been made to the transplanting of Oak I am not knowing enough in this matter to say how far this is true when so young as 2 to 5 or 6 years – The next thing is to be careful to thin the trees for more timber is lost by being too fearful of cutting down than boldly thinning a Tree from 10 years of age ought by a scale given to me by a very able man, to be as follows viz

Number of trees that such land as the Forest of Dean may contain at different periods from their being first sett,

| Trees distant from each other | Years after being set in | No. of Trees an acre | No. of trees to be thinned |
|---|---|---|---|
| 6 | 10 | 1200 | |
| 10 | 20 | 430 | 770 |
| 15 | 40 | 190 | 240 |
| 20 | 60 | 100 | 90 |
| 25 | 80 | 60 | 40 |
| 30 | 100 | 45 | 15 |

In forty years these forests will produce a great value of timber fit for many uses in the Navy indeed all except the Ships of the Line

If on a due consideration it is found not to be practicable for Government to arrainge a plan for growing their own Timber, Then I would recommend at one selling the Forests and encourage the growth of Oak Timber I calculate that taking away the 3500 Load of timber at present fit for cutting (or be it more less) that the Forest of Dean will sell for 460,000£. I am sensible that what I have thrown together on paper is so loose that no plan can be drawn from it but if these facts which I have learnt from my late tour may be in the least degree instrumental in benefitting Our Country I shall be truly happy

After-thoughts on encouraging the growth of oak Timber drawn from conversations with many Gentlemen in my late tour,

1st the reason why Timber has of late years been so much reduced has been uniformly told me that from the pressure of the times gentlemen who had a 1000£ to five-worth of timber on their estates although only half grown (say 50 years of age) were obliged to sell it to raise temporary sums (say to pay Legacys) the Owner cannot, however sorry he may feel to see the beauty of his place destroy'd and what would be treble the value to his children anhilated, help himself

It has struck me forcibly that if the Government could form a plan to purchase of such gentlemen the growing Oak that it would be a National benefit and a great and pleasing accomodation to such growers of Oak as wish to sell

My knowledge of this subject drawn from the conversation of gentlemen in the oak Countries I think would almost obviate all Difficultys, Of myself I own my incompetence to draw up a plan fit for public inspection but all my gathered knowledge shall be most cheerfully at the service of some Able Man

*This report, was written with the left hand, and contains only one full stop in eleven pages – Nelson seeming to prefer the use of commas. He recorded his thoughts as they occurred to him and are here reproduced exactly as they were written down in 1802.*

# APPENDIX B

*The Hamilton & Nelson Papers – Morrison Collection*

Sheets of Accounts (in Lord Nelson's handwriting) dated between July 20th and September 21st 1802 14 pages 4 to

Subscribed by Sir Wm. Hamilton & myself at Merton, July 20th 1802, £100 each, being £200.

| | £ | | |
|---|---|---|---|
| 8 Horses, Merton to Hounslow not paid Mr. Woodman. | 3 | 9 | 4 |
| Horses from Hounslow to Maidenhead | | | |
| From M. to Henly | £ | 2 2 | 0 |
| Benson | £ | 2 11 | 4 |
| Oxford | £ | 2 16 | 0 |
| Bill at the 'Star' Oxford & Servants | £ | 27 0 | 10 |
| Dorton Dresses | £ | 23 2 | 0 |
| University Servts | £ | 1 1 | 0 |
| Horses to Woodstock | £ | 2 0 | 0 |
| Bill at Do. & Servts | £ | 15 2 | 2 |
| Same at Blenheim | £ | 2 2 | 0 |
| Francatello | £ | 1 7 | 0 |
| Horses to Troymill from Burford | £ | 3 14 | 0 |
| To Gloster | £ | 3 5 | 4 |
| Eating at | £ | 0 5 | 0 |
| Bill at Gloster | £ | 6 15 | 9 |
| Same at the | £ | 2 2 | 0 |
| To Ross | £ | 3 14 | 8 |
| Monmouth | £ | 2 8 | 0 |
| Do. by Water | £ | 3 6 | 0 |
| Bill at Ross | £ | 0 19 | 0 |

| | | | | |
|---|---|---|---|---|
| Francatello | £ | 0 | 16 | 0 |
| Bill at Monmouth | £ | 8 | 11 | 10 |
| To Abergavenny | £ | 3 | 14 | 8 |
| Brecon | £ | 4 | 13 | 4 |
| Bill at Brecon | £ | 7 | 13 | 9 |
| To Myrter Tydder | £ | 8 | 8 | 0 |
| Francatello | £ | 0 | 8 | 2 |
| Bill at Myrter Tydder | £ | 6 | 1 | 0 |
| Servts at do. | £ | 1 | 5 | 0 |
| From Brecon to Trecastle | £ | 2 | 11 | 0 |
| Trecastle & Llandovery | £ | 2 | 2 | 0 |
| Bill at do. | £ | 2 | 10 | 2 |
| Servts | £ | 0 | 17 | 6 |
| To Carmarthen 27 m | £ | 6 | 6 | 0 |
| Drivers, turnpikes, gearing etc | £ | 2 | 4 | 0 |
| Playhouse | £ | 3 | 3 | 0 |
| Ventriloquist | £ | 1 | 1 | 0 |
| Bill at Carmarthen & servts | £ | 4 | 3 | 4 |
| St. Clairs for breaft. | £ | 0 | 18 | 0 |
| From Carm. to Narberth 2 pair | £ | 2 | 19 | 0 |
| From Carm. to Har. Wt. 2 pr. | £ | 3 | 4 | 0 |
| Drivers | £ | 0 | 16 | 0 |
| Ringers at Narberth | £ | 1 | 1 | 0 |
| From Narberth to Milford 2 pr. | £ | 2 | 17 | 2 |
| Haverfd Wt to Milford 2 pr. | £ | 1 | 3 | 4 |
| Drivers except to posts from Merton to Milford | £ | 11 | 0 | 6 |

| | | | | |
|---|---|---|---|---|
| Journey to Milford | £189 | 12 | 10 | |

Sir Wm. Hamilton & myself subscribed 30 guineas each on August 5th being £63.

| | | | | |
|---|---|---|---|---|
| Bill at Milford, Breakfast & Servts | £ | 56 | 1 | 5 |
| Dinner & Horses to Picton | £ | 5 | 5 | 0 |
| Oyster Man | £ | | 2 | 6 |
| Boats to Picton | £ | 2 | 2 | 0 |

| | £ | | | |
|---|---|---|---|---|
| Drivers to Picton | £ | | 5 | 0 |
| Coachman | £ | 1 | 1 | 0 |
| Rider | £ | | 7 | 0 |
| Servt. Maids | £ | 1 | 1 | 0 |
| Drivers to Ridgeway | £ | | 6 | 6 |
| Letters | £ | | 1 | 6 |
| Drivers to Stackpole | £ | 1 | 4 | 0 |
| Feed for Horses and Men at Pembroke | £ | | 14 | 0 |
| Return Turnpikes | £ | | 1 | 6 |
| Coachman to Ld.C. | £ | 1 | 1 | 0 |
| Francatello | £ | | 15 | 4 |
| Bill at Tenby | £ | 8 | 7 | 6 |
| Servts. | £ | | 7 | 6 |
| Horses as by bill from Narberth to Stackpole, Pembroke Tenby & St. Clairs. | £ | 14 | 4 | 4 |
| Drivers | £ | 1 | 8 | 0 |
| Turnpikes paid by Drivers | £ | | 1 | 6 |
| Bill at St. Clairs | £ | 3 | 12 | 10 |
| Servts | £ | | 7 | 0 |
| Ostler | £ | | 2 | 0 |
| Horses to Carthn. | £ | 2 | 2 | 0 |
| Drivers | £ | | 10 | 6 |
| From Carthen to Lennon | £ | 2 | 16 | 0 |
| Drivers | £ | | 12 | 6 |
| To Clairmont | £ | 3 | 0 | 0 |
| Drivers | £ | | 12 | 0 |
| Ringers | £ | 2 | 2 | 0 |
| Greasing the Carriages | £ | | 3 | 0 |
| Bill for Horses at Swansey; yesterday to Pyll | £ | 7 | 0 | 0 |
| Drivers | £ | | 16 | 0 |
| Gardner at Magorn | £ | | 3 | 0 |
| From Pyll to Yewbridge & Servts & eating | £ | 3 | 8 | 8 |
| Drivers | £ | | 12 | 0 |
| To Cardiff | £ | 3 | 0 | 0 |
| Drivers & Turnpikes | £ | | 16 | 0 |
| Francatello | £ | 1 | 3 | 0 |
| Bill at Cardiff incldg Horses to Newport | £ | 7 | 15 | 9 |

93

| | | | |
|---|---|---:|---:|
| Drivers | £ | 12 | 0 |
| From Newport to Chepstow | £ | 4 0 | 0 |
| Drivers | £ | 14 | 0 |
| Bill at Chepstow | £ | 2 10 | 0 |
| Servts. | £ | 7 | 0 |
| Reps to Carriage | £ | 2 | 6 |
| Horses to Monmouth | £ | 4 15 | 0 |
| Drivers | £ | 16 | 0 |
| Francatello | £ | 18 | 0 |
| Bill at Monmouth incldg Servts | £ | 4 15 | 0 |
| Horses to the Kymin & to Reedhall | £ | 3 11 | 0 |
| Drivers | £ | 16 | 0 |
| Ross Bill for Horses to Hereford | | | |
| & 2 pr to Leominster & Drivers | £ | 6 15 | 0 |
| Horses 2 pr from Hereford to Leominster | £ | 2 6 | 6 |
| Horses from Leominster to Ludlow | £ | 2 10 | 0 |
| Drivers & Turnpikes and Drivers from | £ | 1 1 | 0 |
| Hereford | | | |
| Eating at Leominster | £ | 1 1 | 0 |
| | | | |
| | £170 14 2 | | |

| | | | |
|---|---|---:|---:|
| Bill at Ludlow for going to Downton | £ | 5 19 | 0 |
| returning to Tenbury & Repairs to Coach | | | |
| Drivers to Downton & | £ | 16 | 0 |
| Do. to Tenbury | £ | 10 | 6 |
| Turnpikes | £ | 6 | 0 |
| Horses to Hundred House | £ | 2 16 | 0 |
| Drivers | £ | 12 | 0 |
| Turnpikes | £ | 2 | 0 |
| To Worcester | £ | 2 11 | 4 |
| Drivers | £ | 12 | 0 |
| Bill at Worcester | £ | 4 7 | 8 |
| Servants | £ | 1 5 | 6 |
| Francatello | £ | 1 12 | 6 |
| Cyder & Perry | £ | 12 16 | 10 |

| | | | | |
|---|---|---:|---:|---:|
| From Worcester to Broomsgrove | £ | 3 | 0 | 8 |
| Drivers | £ | | 12 | 0 |
| Ostler | £ | | 2 | 0 |
| Horses to Birmingham | £ | 3 | 0 | 10 |
| Drivers | £ | | 12 | 0 |
| Bill at Birmingham | £ | 8 | 16 | 10 |
| Men Servts. | £ | 1 | 11 | 6 |
| Female do. | £ | 1 | 10 | 0 |
| Bootcleaners | £ | | 2 | 6 |
| Francatello's Bill for Washing | £ | 5 | 0 | 0 |
| Horses to Hockley – paid wrong | £ | 2 | 18 | 0 |
| Drivers | £ | | 12 | 0 |
| Ostler | £ | | 4 | 0 |
| To Warwick | £ | 2 | 6 | 8 |
| Drivers | £ | | 12 | 0 |
| Turnpikes | £ | | 6 | 0 |
| Bill at Warwick | £ | 9 | 15 | 0 |
| Male Servts. | £ | 1 | 1 | 0 |
| Female do. | £ | | 10 | 6 |
| Bootcleaners | £ | | 2 | 0 |
| Ostler | £ | | 4 | 0 |
| Horses to Coventry | £ | 2 | 6 | 8 |
| Drivers | £ | | 10 | 8 |
| Turnpikes | £ | | 2 | 0 |
| Bill at Coventry | £ | 1 | 1 | 0 |
| Horses to Danchurch | £ | 2 | 11 | 4 |
| Drivers | £ | | 12 | 0 |
| Turnpikes | £ | | 3 | 0 |
| To Daintree | £ | 1 | 17 | 4 |
| Drivers | £ | | 10 | 6 |
| To Tocester | £ | 2 | 16 | 0 |
| Drivers | £ | | 12 | 0 |
| Ostlers | £ | | 2 | 0 |
| Bill at Towcester | £ | 1 | 6 | 0 |
| Servts. | £ | | 5 | 0 |
| Horses to Sy Stratford | £ | 1 | 17 | 4 |
| Drivers | £ | | 10 | 6 |

| | | | |
|---|---|--:|--:|
| Ostlers | £ | 2 | 0 |
| To Brisley | £ 2 | 2 | 0 |
| Drivers | £ | 10 | 6 |
| Ostler | £ | 1 | 0 |
| To Dunstable | £ 2 | 6 | 8 |
| Drivers | £ | 11 | 4 |
| Francatello's Bill | £ 1 | 7 | 0 |
| Bill at Dunstable | £ 2 | 14 | 8 |
| Male Servts. | £ | 15 | 0 |
| Female Do. | £ | 7 | 0 |
| Ostler | £ | 4 | 0 |
| Bootcleaner | £ | 2 | 0 |
| Horses to St. Albans | £ 3 | 5 | 0 |
| Drivers | £ | 12 | 0 |
| Ostlers | £ | 2 | 0 |
| | | | |
| | £109 11 | | 2 |
| | | | |
| | | | |
| Horses to Watford | £ 2 | 0 | 0 |
| Drivers | £ | 10 | 6 |
| Ostlers | £ | 1 | 0 |
| To Brentford | £ 4 | 0 | 0 |
| Drivers | £ | 14 | 0 |
| To Merton (11 miles) | £ 2 | 15 | 0 |
| Drivers | £ | 12 | 0 |
| Bridge | £ | 1 | 6 |
| Francatello | £ | 11 | 8 |
| | | | |
| | £ 11 5 | | 8 |
| | £189 12 | | 10 |
| | £170 14 | | 2 |
| | £109 11 | | 2 |
| | | | |
| | £481 3 | | 10 |

# Bibliography

Binns, R.W.           *A Century of Pottery in the City of Worcester* (1866)

Briggs, Asa           *The Age of Improvement 1783–1867* (1959)

Byng, John (ed.)      *The Torrington Diaries* (1974)

Chamberlain, W.H.     *Reminiscences of Old Merton* (1925)

Clarke, T.E.          *A Guide to Merthyr Tydfil* (1848)

Cliffe, Charles F     *The Book of South Wales, the Bristol Channel, Monmouthshire and the Wye* (1848)

Cobbett, William      *Rural Rides* (1830)

Cox, G.V.             *Recollections of Oxford* (1868)

Dent, R.K.            *Old and New Birmingham* (1880)

Druce, Fred           *A Good Plain Country Town, Ross on Wye 1800–1930* (Ross on Wye 1980)

Fenton, Richard       *Historical Tour in Pembrokeshire* (1811)

Freeman, E.C.         *Historic Haverfordwest* (1960)

Freeman, E.C. and     *Nelson and the Hamiltons in Wales and Mon-*
Gill, Edward          *mouthshire* (1962)

Gill, Conrad          *History of Birmingham* (1952)

Gwilliam, H.W.        *Old Worcester People and Places* (Worcester, 1975)

Hall, Mr. and         *Book of South Wales, the Wye and the Coast*
Mrs. S.C.             (1861)

Harrison, James       *The Life of the Right Honourable Horatio, Lord Viscount Nelson* (1806), 2 vols.

Hardwick, Mollie      *Emma, Lady Hamilton* (1969)

Heath, Charles        *Descriptive Account of the Kymin Pavilion. Proud Days for Monmouth, Lord Nelson's Visit* (Monmouth, 1802)

Heath, Charles        *A General Description of the County of Monmouth* (1804)

| | |
|---|---|
| Hughes, John Vivian | *Some Visitors to Margam* (1977) |
| Inglis-Jones, E. | *Peacocks in Paradise* (1950) |
| Kissack, Keith | *Monmouth – The Making of A County Town* (1975) |
| Kissack, Keith | *The River Wye* (Lavenham, 1978) |
| Langford, J.A. | *A Century of Birmingham Life 1741–1841* (1868) |
| Lofts, Norah | *Emma Hamilton* (New York, 1978) |
| Mackenzie, R.H. | *Trafalgar Roll* (1913) |
| Marshall, Edward | *The Early History of Woodstock Manor and its Environs* (1873) |
| Matcham, M. Eyre | *The Nelsons of Burnham Thorpe* (1911) |
| Minto, Countess of (ed.) | *Life and Letters of Sir Gilbert Elliot, First Earl of Minto, from 1751 to 1806* (1874), 3 vols. |
| Moore, Patricia | *Margam Orangery* (1986) |
| Moorhouse, E. Hallam | *Nelson in England* (1913) |
| Morrison, Alfred (ed.) | *Autograph Letters and Historical Documents: the Hamilton and Nelson Papers* (privately printed 1893–4), 2 vols. |
| Nance, E.M. | *The Pottery and Porcelain of Swansea and Nantgarw* (1942) |
| Nicholas, Sir N.H. | *Dispatches and Letters of Vice-Admiral Lord Viscount Nelson* (1844–6), 7 vols |
| Oman, Carola | *Nelson* (1974) |
| Pollock, Sir F. (ed.) | *Macready's Reminiscences and Selections from his Diaries and Letters* (1875) |
| Price, Cecil | *English Theatre in Wales* (Cardiff, 1948) |
| Rayner, Eric | *Discovering the Gloucester Road* |
| Rees, Sir Frederick | *The Story of Milford* (Cardiff, 1954) |
| Ruff, H. | *History of Cheltenham and its Environs* (Cheltenham, 1803) |
| Russell, Jack | *Nelson and The Hamiltons* (1969) |
| Spurrell, William | *Carmarthen and its Neighbourhood* (Carmarthen, 1879) |

| Stebbings and Shaw | *History and Antiquities of Staffordshire* (1798–1801) |
| Stewart Taylor, M | *The Crawshays of Cyfartha Castle* (1960) |
| Warner, Oliver | *Emma Hamilton and Sir William* (1960) |
| Misc. Authors | *Swansea Guide* (Swansea, 1802) |

# Notes and References

1. British Museum, Egerton MS. II, 240, 151
2. A. Morrison (ed.), *Autograph Letters and Historical Documents: The Hamilton and Nelson Papers* (privately printed in two volumes 1893–4), document number 638 (hereafter referred to simply as Morrison MS, followed by the document reference). See also Carola Oman, *Nelson* (1947), p. 482.
3. Minto, Countess of (ed.), *Life and Letters of Sir Gilbert Elliot, First Earl of Minto, from 1757 to 1806* (1874), Vol. 3, p.242.
4. Morrison MS 684.
5. Morrison MS Appendix D, p. 408.
6. Morrison MS 136
7. O. Warner, *Emma Hamilton and Sir William* (1960).
8. Ibid.
9. Morrison MS 150.
10. Warner, op. cit.
11. Morrison MSS 152 and 153.
12. Morrison MSS 152 and 153.
13. Morrison MS 157.
14. Warner, op. cit.
15. Morrison MS Appendix C, pp. 401–404. Printed in full in the Appendix to this book.
16. Morrison MS Appendix C, p. 401.
17. M.E. Matcham *The Nelsons of Burnham Thorpe*, (1911), p. 201.
18. *Jackson's Oxford Journal*, 24 July 1802.
19. G.V. Cox, *Recollections of Oxford* (1868).
20. E. Marshall *The Early History of Woodstock Manor and Its Environs* (1873), pp. 46–7.
21. J. Harrison, *The Life of the Right Honourable Horatio, Lord Viscount Nelson* (1806).
22. H. Ruff, *History of Cheltenham and Its Environs* (1803).
23. *Gloucester Journal*, 2 August 1802.
24. Original MS in Nelson Museum, Monmouth.
25. *Gloucester Journal* – 2 August 1802. The Swan Inn, Ross on Wye is not the existing Swan Inn, but what was known as the Swan and Falcon, now No. 4, High St.
26. *Gloucester Journal*, 2 August 1802.

27.  Charles Heath, *A Descriptive Account of The Kymin Pavilion* (1802).

28.  *Dictionary of National Biography*

29.  J. Harrison, op. cit.

30.  The Brecon poet, William Churchey, published this elegy on Nelson in 1802.

31.  The letter from Nelson to Churchey, mentioned in Poole's *History of Brecon*, was purchased for £185 in a Sotheby's sale in the 1960s by Mr. L. T. Edwards, a former High Sheriff who presented it to the town's museum.

32.  M. Hardwick, *Emma, Lady Hamilton* (1969)

33.  *Gloucester Journal*, 2 August 1802.

34.  T. E. Clarke, *A Guide to Merthyr Tydfil* (1848).

35.  *Gloucester Journal*, 2 August 1802.

36.  C. Price, *English Theatre In Wales* (1948).

37.  W. Spurrell, *History of Carmarthen* (1879).

38.  Harrison, op. cit.

39.  Morrison MS 651.

40.  Harrison, op.cit.

41.  J. F. Rees, *The Story of Milford*. Jean-Louis Barrallier was a native of Toulon. A prominent counter-revolutionary, he actively co-operated with the British during the three months of occupation in 1793. He left with the British and after some service in the Mediterranean, settled in Milford with his family in 1797. He was appointed Inspector General of Construction, and played an important part in Greville's Milford scheme.

42.  Harrison, op.cit.

43.  Sir N. H. Nicholas, *Dispatches and Letters of Vice-Admiral Lord Viscount Nelson* (1844–6).

44.  In 1603, the Pembrokeshire writer George Owen recorded: 'The oysters in auncient time were accompted seasonable in those moneths onely that had R but experience nowe teacheth that in May, June July and August there are some found to be very sweete and wholesome.'

45.  Some years ago, Eric Freeman rescued this historic document from obscurity when it was auctioned by Sotheby's and subsequently returned it to Haverfordwest.

46.  E. H. Moorhouse, *Nelson in England* (1913).

47.  *Hereford News and Journal*, 27 August 1802.

48.  C. Price, *English Theatre in Wales* (1948).

49.  Mr. Gore's apparently peculiar reference to the Spanish Dollar would not have been out of place in Nelson's day. Spanish treasure ships were fair game for the British navy, and held rich rewards for the Government as well as the seamen. Because of the scarcity of gold and silver, the Bank of England issued Spanish dollars

101

captured from these treasure ships as legal currency, having first impressed the head of King George III on the bust of the King of Spain.

50.  W. H. Jones, *Miscellaneous Notes On Swansea.* (Recollections of his grandfather), p. 138; MS in Swansea City Library.

51.  MS of E. E. Rowse, Swansea City Library.

52.  In Col. R. H. Mackenzie's *Trafalgar Roll*, Lewis Rotley is listed as a Marine Officer serving on HMS *Victory*.

53.  In a letter to Edward Gill dated 19.8.74, the National Maritime Museum confirmed that the breeches and socks were bequeathed to Greenwich Hospital by Miss Jane Roteley in 1896. They are now on permanent display.

54.  E. M. Nance, *The Pottery and Porcelain of Swansea and Nantgarw* (1942), pp. 81 and 82.

55.  C. F. Cliffe, *The Book of South Wales, the Bristol Channel, Monmouthshire and The Wye* (1848).

56.  John Vivian Hughes, 'Thomas Mansel Talbot of Margam & Penrice (1747–1813)' *Gower Journal*, Vol. 26 1975.

57.  J. V. Hughes, *Margam Park, Glamorgan.*

58.  This plaque was unveiled on Trafalgar Day in 1961 by Mrs. Horatia Durant, a great-great-grand-daughter of Lord Nelson and Emma Hamilton.

59.  C. Heath, *A General Description of the County of Monmouth* (1804).

60.  The details of Nelson's visits to Monmouth have been taken from the eye witness accounts of Charles Heath in his book *Descriptive Accounts of the Kymin Pavilion and Naval Temple*, first printed and published by the author in 1802.

61.  Ibid. Because, to my knowledge, it has not been reprinted since Heath's time, almost the whole of the account of Nelson's Monmouth visit is printed exactly as he wrote it.

62.  The letter from James Davies to Lord Gage is in the Gage Papers at Gloucester Record Office. The Buckstone referred to in the letter is a well known natural stone landmark near the Kymin, said, without any certainty to have had druidical origins.

63.  The accounts of the Rudhall and Hereford visits were taken from Heath's *Descriptive Account of the Kymin and Naval Temple*, and the *Hereford News and Journal* of 27 August 1802. Details of the Westfaling family and Rudhall Manor are taken from *Woolhope Trans.* 1914, p. 20.

64.  *Morning Post*, 17 August 1802.

65.  *Dictionary of National Biography.*

66.  *Morning Post*, 1 September 1802.

67.  *Hereford News and Journal*, August 1802.

68.  Original MS in Hereford Record Office.

69. E. Inglis-Jones, *Peacocks in Paradise* (1950) and Browne and Burton, *Worthies of Worcestershire.*
70. Morrison MS 682.
71. Morrison MS 680.
72. Morrison MS 466.
73. C. Oman, *Nelson* (1947), p. 630.
74. *Berrows Worcester Journal*, August 1802.
75. H. W. Gwilliam, *Old Worcester People and Places* (1975).
76. R. W. Binns, *A Century of Pottery in the City of Worcester.*
77. *Berrows Worcester Journal*, August 1802.
78. Gwilliam, op.cit.
79. *Coventry Mercury*, 6 September 1802.
80. Ibid.
81. Sir F. Pollock, *Macready's Reminiscences and Selections from his Diaries and Letters.*
82. *Coventry Mercury*, 6 September 1802.
83. Ibid.
84. Moorhouse, op.cit.
85. Minto, Countess of, op. cit.. Vol. 3, p. 363.
86. Carola Oman (in Oman, op. cit.) says that the original MS is in Somerset House.

# Index

ABERAVON 44
ABERGAVENNY 23, 24
ABOUKIR 16, 33
ALTHORP PARK
(Northamptonshire) 72, 80
AMIENS, Treaty of 2, 76
*AMPHION*, HMS 82
ANKER, Baron 62
APRILE, Giuseppe 57
ARUNDEL (Sussex) 63, 79

BADMINTON
(Gloucestershire) 54
BARLOW, Katherine, *see* Hamilton, Katherine
BARLOW (family of Slebech) 81
BARRALLIER, Jean Louis 35
BATEMAN-PRUST, Robert 38
BATH 14, 19
BATH, Order of 4, 15
BEAUFORT ARMS INN
(Monmouth) 23, 51
BEAUFORT, Duchess of 52

BEAUFORT, Duke of 54
BECKFORD, William 79
BENNETT'S HOTEL
(Hereford) 63
BIRMINGHAM 72, 75–9
BLENHEIM PALACE 15, 16, 31
BLISSET, Mr. (actor) 76
BLUE BOAR INN (St Clears) 32
BLUE COAT SCHOOL
(Birmingham) 79
BOND STREET (London) 69
BOSCAWEN, Admiral 52
BOULTON, Matthew 79
BOWOOD HOUSE
(Wiltshire) 67
BRECON 23, 25, 26, 29, 50
BRERETON, Thomas, *see* Westfaling
BRIDPORT (Dorset) 16
BRISTOL 35, 48, 72
BROMSGROVE
(Worcestershire) 72, 75
BROMYARD
(Herefordshire) 69
BRONTË, Duke of 4, 15, 40

BRONTË, Sicilian
   Commune of 4
BROWN, Capability 67
BUCKSTONE, Monmouth
   53
BULKELEY (Sr), Richard
   68, 69, 70
BULKELEY (Jr), Richard
   (Dick) 69, 70
BULL INN (Burford) 17
BURFORD (Oxfordshire)
   13, 16, 17
BYNG, John (Hon. 5th
   Visc. Torrington) 19

CALAIS 84, 85
CALVI 36
*CAMBRIAN* (Newspaper) 41
CARDIFF 33, 46
CARMARTHEN 23, 30, 31,
   32, 41
CARVER, Colonel 78
CASTLE INN (Llandovery)
   30
CAWDOR, Earl of 39, 67
CHAMBERLAIN Porcelain
   Factory 73, 74
CHARLES II 17
CHELTENHAM 16
CHEPSTOW
   (Monmouthshire) 47, 48
CHURCHEY, Walter (Poet)
   25, 26
CHURCHILL, Winston 57
CLASEMONT HOUSE 42, 68
CLAY, Mr. (Japanware
   Mfr) 78

CLEAVES, Tom (of
   Swansea) 42
COALBROOKDALE 67
COBBETT, William 17, 20
COLES & HAYNES POTTERY
   (Swansea) 43
CONWAY, Anne (dr of
   F.M. Conway) 8
COPENHAGEN, Battle of 3,
   24, 30, 34, 54, 57, 62
COVENTRY (Warwickshire)
   72, 80
COVENTRY, Earl of 74
*COVENTRY MERCURY* (News-
   paper) 75, 77
COWBRIDGE, Glamorgan
   46
COWPER, Lord 68
COX, G.V. (of Oxford) 15
CRAWSHAY, Richard
   (ironmaster) 27, 29, 62
CRIBB, Thomas 83
CRICKHOWELL
   (Breconshire) 23, 24, 25
CROWN INN (Ludlow) 66
CYFARTHA IRONWORKS
   (Merthyr) 27, 29

DAVENTRY 72
DAVIES, John 53
DAVISON, Alexander 2, 80
DEAL (Kent) 35
DEAN, Forest of 18, 19, 20,
   53, 86–90
DEVAUDEN 48
DIGBY, Capt. R.N. 78
DOMESDAY BOOK 17

DOWNTON CASTLE (Herefordshire) 47, 66, 67
DROITWICH (Worcestershire) 72, 75
DUNSTABLE (Bedfordshire) 72, 80

EDGEWARE ROW 8, 9
EGINTON, Mr. (Stained Glass Mfr) 78
*ELEPHANT*, HMS 34, 35
ELLIS, Will (seaman of Merthyr) 28
ERMIN STREET 18
ETNA, Mount 4
EVANS, 'Admiral' (Ross on Wye) 21

FEATHERSTONHAUGH, Sir Harry 8
FERDINAND (King of Naples) 4
FOLEY, Emily (dr of John) 39
FOLEY, John of Ridgeway 38, 39
FOLEY, Capt. Thomas 34, 35, 38, 39
FFORESTFACH (Swansea) 41
FONTHILL (Wiltshire) 79
FOSSE WAY 17
FRANCATELLO (Neopolitan servant) 14
FROGMILL INN Gloucestershire, 13, 17

GAETANO, Spedilo (valet) 14
GAGE, Lord 53
GELL, Admiral John 24, 25
GLAMORGAN, West County Council 45
GLASS, Rev. Herbert of Pencombe 69
GLOUCESTER 2, 13, 18, 19
*GLOUCESTER JOURNAL* 60
GLOUCESTER ROYAL MAIL 17
GÖETHE 66
GOODRICH CASTLE (Herefordshire) 21
GORE, Mr. (of Tenby) 40, 41
GUZZARDI, Palermo (artist) 37
GWYNNE, Nell 17

HALLOWELL, Capt. Benjamin 37, 84
HAMILTON, Lady Emma (*see also* Hart, Emma, *and* Lyon, Amy *or* Emily): meets Nelson 1; at Merton 2–7; threatens Greville 11; marries Sir William 12; 13, 14, 16, 17, 27, 29, 31, 39, 40, 41, 44, 48, 54, 58, 60, 62, 63, 66–9, 73–5, 77, 81, 82, 83; flees to Calais and dies there 84; British

106

soldiers raise memorial 85

HAMILTON, Katherine, 1st Lady 81

HAMILTON, Sir William: meets Nelson 1; at Merton 2–7; corresponds with Greville over Emma 8–12; marries Emma 12; pilgrimage to Slebech 13, 14, 15, 16, 17, 25, 27, 32, 33, 34, 36, 37, 38; dies in Emma's arms 40, 42, 44, 45, 57, 58, 61, 62, 66, 67, 68, 69, 73, 75, 80, 81; will 82

HARDWICK, Mr. (of Monmouth) 52

HARDY, Capt. Thomas Masterman 70

HART, Emma (*see also* Hamilton) 9

HAVERFORDWEST (Pembrokeshire) 32, 33, 38

HEATH, Charles (of Monmouth) 21, 49, 50, 51, 52, 54, 55, 56, 57, 58, 59, 60, 61

HENEAGE-LEGGE, Mr. (of Birmingham) 78

HENLEY-ON-THAMES 13, 14

HENRY V 22, 61

HEREFORD 47, 56, 62, 63, 64, 65, 66

HEREFORD, Bishop of 66

*HEREFORD NEWS & JOURNAL* 60

*HICHINGBROOKE*, HMS 69

HIGGS-BARKER, Rev. Wm. (Carmarthen) 31

HOLLINGS, Thos. (Mayor of Monmouth) 24, 50

HOLME LACEY (Herefordshire) 63

HOOD, Sir Samuel 37

HOP POLE INN (Worcester) 72

HOUNSLOW 13, 14

HYDE PARKER, Sir 34

IVY BUSH INN (Carmarthen) 32

JENKINS, Miss (of Merthyr Tydfil) 27, 28

JERUSALEM, Knights of St. John of 38

JOHNSON, Dr. Samuel 18, 19

KENSINGTON, Lord 41

KING'S ARMS INN (Carmarthen) 41

KING'S BENCH, Court of 84

KING'S HEAD INN (Coventry) 80

KING'S HEAD INN (Gloucester) 18

KNIGHT, Miss Cornelia 55

KYMIN, The (Monmouth) 22, 50, 51, 52, 53

KYMIN CLUB (Monmouth) 51

LAMB, Mr. Lacon (Hereford) 64
LANDOR, Walter Savage 44
LANSDOWN, Lord 67
LEGHORN (Italy) 45
LEOMINSTER (Herefordshire) 47, 66
LINDSAY, Hon. John (of Monmouth) 56, 58
LION INN (Tenby) 41
LLANARTHNEY TOWER (Carmarthen) 30
LLANDEILO (Carmarthenshire) 30
LLANDOGER TROW (Bristol) 48
LLANDOVERY (Carmarthenshire) 23, 30
LLANGATTOCK, Lady Georgiana 50
LLANGWM 38
LLANWYSG (Crickhowell) 24
LLEWELLYN, Dr. William (of Margam) 46
LONDON 12, 14, 25, 31, 36, 39, 57, 62, 63, 81
L'ORIENT (French flagship) 5, 37, 84
LORDS, House of 4, 76
LUDLOW (Shropshire) 47, 66, 67, 68, 70

LYON, Amy or Emily (see also Hamilton, Lady Emma) 1, 102

MACKWORTH ARMS HOTEL (Swansea) 42
MACREADY, W.C. (actor) 76, 77
MAGDALEN BRIDGE (Oxford) 14
MAHAN, Col. (7th Dragoon Guards) 78
MAIDENHEAD (Berkshire) 13, 14
MALVERN HILLS (Worcestershire) 50
MARGAM (Glamorgan) 33, 44, 45, 46
MARLBOROUGH, Geo. Spencer, 4th Duke of 15, 16, 29
MARYLEBONE 12
MASTERMAN, Henry (actor manager) 31
MATCHAM, George 14, 19, 82, 83
MATCHAM, Kitty (née Nelson) 2, 14, 19, 82, 83
MATTHEWS, Charles (entertainer) 31
MERTHYR TYDFIL 23, 27, 28, 29, 41, 62
MERTON PLACE (Surrey) 2, 3–7, 13, 19, 39, 60, 68, 72, 80, 81, 82, 83, 84
MILFORD HAVEN (Pembrokeshire) 7, 8,

12, 13, 14, 26, 32, 33–7, 68, 80

MILFORD, Lord 37, 38

MINTO, Gilbert Elliott, 1st Earl 4, 5, 6, 40, 82

MONMOUTH 21, 22, 23, 24, 47, 48, 49, 50, 51–61, 67, 68

MONMOUTH & BRECON MILITIA 23

*MORNING POST* (newspaper) 25, 62, 63

MORRIS, Mr. John (ironmaster) 27, 42, 68

NAPLES 1, 2, 10, 12, 38, 44, 45, 57, 61, 73

NARBERTH (Pembrokeshire) 32

NASH, John (architect) 25, 39

NATIONAL MARITIME MUSEUM 43, 50

NATIONAL TRUST 30, 51, 52

NELSON, Rev. Edmund 15

NELSON, Horatia 3, 39, 82, 83, 84

NELSON, Horatio Vice-Admiral Lord (*see also* Duke of Brontë) buys Merton 1–6; at Oxford 12, 13, 14, 15; Marlborough's rebuff 16; at Gloucester 17; at Monmouth 19, 20, 21, 23–24; visits Admiral

Gell 25; at Merthyr 26, 27–30; at Milford 32–7; tours Pembrokeshire 38–41; visits Swansea and Margam 42–5; Cardiff and Newport, Chepstow and Piersfield 46–50; fêted at Monmouth 51–61; at Rudhall 61–62; at Hereford 63–6; Ludlow, Downton, Pencombe and Tenbury 66–70; at Worcester 72–5; visits Birmingham 76–8; at Warwick and Coventry 79; visits Lord Spencer 80; mobbed by admirers in London 81–2; last hours with Emma and Horatia at Merton 83; death and burial in St. Paul's Cathedral 83–4; Forest of Dean report 86–90

NELSON, Horatio (son of Rev. Wm.) 14

NELSON HOTEL (Milford Haven) 37 (*see also* New Inn)

NELSON MUSEUM (Monmouth) 49, 50

NELSON, Rev. Dr. William (*see also* Trafalgar, 1st Earl) 14, 15, 43, 61, 77, 82, 84

NESTON (Cheshire) 1

NEW INN (Milford Haven) 32, 37 (*see also* Nelson Hotel)

NEWPORT (Monmouthshire) 46

NILE, Battle of 13, 22, 24, 33, 37, 40, 52, 54, 57, 65

NORFOLK, Charles Howard, 11th Duke 63, 64, 79

NORTH Dudley 63

NORTHLEACH 17

OXFORD 2, 13, 14, 15, 29

OXFORD UNIVERSITY 15

PARRY, Mr. Henry (of Monmouth) 57

PAXTON, Sir William 30

PAYNE KNIGHT, Richard (of Downton) 66, 67, 68, 69

PEMBROKE 13, 39, 81

PEMBROKESHIRE (French invasion) 39

PEMBROKESHIRE Royal Militia Band 38

PENCOMBE (Herefordshire) 47, 69, 70

PEPYS, Samuel 20

PICCADILLY (London) 74, 81, 82

PICTON CASTLE (Pembrokeshire) 33, 37, 38

PIERSFIELD PARK

(Chepstow) 48

PITT, William 2

PLANT, James 73

PLUME OF FEATHERS INN (Swansea) 42

PORTSMOUTH 7, 35, 42, 82, 83

PRICE, Sir Uvedale 67

PYLE INN (Glamorgan) 46

RADENHURST (Whip Makers, Birmingham) 79

*REDOUBTABLE* (French ship) 43

RIDGEWAY (Pembrokeshire) 33, 39

ROLLS, C.S. (of Monmouth) 50

ROMNEY, George (artist) 2

ROSS ON WYE (Herefordshire) 13, 19–22, 61, 62

ROTELEY (Sr), Lewis (of Swansea) 42

ROTELEY (Jr), Lewis (of Swansea) 42, 43, 70

ROTELEY, Miss Jean (of Swansea) 43

ROWLANDS, Mr. (Merthyr Parish Clerk) 28

ROYAL HOSPITAL Greenwich 43

ROYAL SOCIETY OF ARTS 63, 81

RUDHALL MANOR (Ross on Wye) 61, 62

RUFUS, William 38
'RULE BRITANNIA' 23, 28, 43, 57, 76

ST. ALBANS (Hertfordshire) 72, 80
ST. ARVANS (Monmouthshire) 48
ST. CLAIRS (Carmarthenshire) 23, 32, 41
*ST. GEORGE*, HMS 34
ST. PAUL'S CATHEDRAL 84
ST. VINCENT, Cape 59
SAN JUAN River Expedition 69
*SANTIAGO* (Spanish treasure ship) 25
SANTISSIMA TRINIDADA 59
SCUDAMORE, Miss Frances 63
SEVEN SISTERS ROCKS (Wye Valley) 22
SEVERN River 18, 35, 48, 49
SHAKESPEARE, William 37, 76
SHELDONIAN THEATRE (Oxford) 15
SHERIDAN, Richard Brinsley 3
SIMCOX & TIMKINS (of Birmingham) 78
SLEBECH (Pembrokeshire) 37, 38, 40, 81
SMITH (Birmingham button maker) 78

SOHO FOUNDRY (Birmingham) 79
SOUTHEY, Robert (poet) 25
SPENCER, George, 2nd Earl of (First Lord of The Admiralty) 35, 80
STACKHOUSE-ACTON, Mrs. 66
STACKPOLE COURT (Pembrokeshire) 33, 39
STAR INN (Merthyr Tydfil) 27
STAR INN (Oxford) 14
STRATFORD-DUGDALE (Dugdale) 78
STYLES HOTEL (Birmingham) 75, 78
SWAN INN (Ross on Wye) 20
SWANSEA (Glamorganshire) 33, 41–4, 68, 70
*SWIFTSURE*, HMS 37
SYMONDS YAT (Herefordshire) 21

TALBOT, Thomas Mansel 44, 45
TEME, River 66, 69, 70
TENBURY WELLS (Worcestershire) 47, 70
TENBY (Pembrokeshire) 33, 40, 41
THAMES, River 81
THREE CRANES INN (Chepstow) 47

111

THREE TUNS INN
(Carmarthen) 32
*TIMES* 2
TIMMINS & JORDAN (of
Birmingham) 78
TINTERN ABBEY
(Monmouthshire) 48
TOULON 25
TOWCESTER
(Northamptonshire) 72,
80
TOWY, River 31
TRAFALGAR, Battle of 30,
42, 70, 74, 79, 83
TRAFALGAR, William, 1st
Earl (*see also* Rev.
William Nelson) 84
TRECASTLE (Breconshire)
30
TRELECH
(Monmouthshire) 48
'TRIA JUNCTA IN UNO' 4,
81
TRINCOMALEE (East
Indies) 35

USK, River
(Monmouthshire) 24, 46

VESUVIUS, Mt. 44
*VICTORY*, HMS (Nelson's
flagship) 43, 47, 70, 82,
83

WALES, Diana, Princess of
80
WARWICK 72, 79
WARWICK, Earl of 7, 79
WARWICK, Elizabeth,
Countess of 79
WARWICK ARMS INN 79
WATKINS, Mr. (of
Monmouth) 23, 24
WATLING STREET 80
WEAVER, Mr. (of
Worcester) 73
WELLS, Mr. & Mrs.
Nathaniel 48
WESTFALING, Mr. & Mrs.
Thomas 61
WITNEY (Oxfordshire) 16
WOLLEY & DEAKINS (sword
makers) 78
WOLSEY, Cardinal 84
WOODSTOCK
(Oxfordshire) 13, 15
WORCESTER 47, 72–5
WYE, River 20, 21, 23, 46,
48, 49, 51, 53, 59, 61
WYE VALLEY 21, 48
WYNDCLIFFE
(Monmouthshire) 48

*ZEALOUS*, HMS 37